# THE MCDOUGALL HEALTH-SUPPORTING COOKBOOK

## VOLUME TWO

### Mary McDougall

## NEW WIN PUBLISHING, INC.

# Acknowledgments

Contributions of recipes and meal ideas from so many of you made this volume a special collection of new and different tastes. Without your input, recipe designing would certainly be less interesting for me. A special thanks for my husband's never-tiring two-finger typing on his never-failing IBM computer.

Printing Code

93  94  95  29  28  27  26  25

**Library of Congress Cataloging-in-Publication Data**
(Revised for vol. 2)

McDougall, Mary A. (Mary Ann)
   The McDougall health-supporting cookbook.

   Includes indexes.
   1. Vegetarianism.   2. Complex carbohydrate diet—Recipes.   3. Salt-free diet—Recipes.   4. Diet therapy.
RM236.M39 1985        641.5′636        85–5056
ISBN 0-8329-0422-8 (pbk. : v. 2)

# Dedication

To my three children, full of life and good health. Each day Craig, Patrick, and Heather reaffirm for me the value of my efforts to provide health-supporting meals for my family.

# CONTENTS

# A BRIEF SUMMARY OF THE MCDOUGALL PLAN

**The McDougall Plan** encourages you to adopt the diet and lifestyle which best supports your natural tendencies to heal and stay healthy. This supportive environment is based around proper foods, moderate exercise, adequate sunshine, pure air and water, and surroundings comfortable to the psychological well being.

The primary component, the diet, is centered around a variety of starchy plant foods such as rice, potatoes and pastas with the addition of fresh or frozen fruits and vegetables. Animal-derived foods and plant products that are refined or otherwise processed are not health supporting and are placed in a category called delicacies. Other plant foods that are also considered delicacies are those high in fat such as nuts, seeds and avocados; and foods high in unprotected simple sugars; for example honey, molasses, and maple syrup. These delicacy foods are to be reserved for special occasions and consumed only by healthy individuals. There are relative degrees of harmfulness among the delicacies. No portions are recommended for the meal plan except that a starch should provide most of the calories. The quantity consumed each day is variable among individuals and governed by our highly efficient hunger drive. Foods that support your health combine to make the most interesting and delicious meals you can imagine.

Additions and modifications of the basic meal plan include:

1) Supplementation of a non-animal source of vitamin B-12 after three years on the plan or if you are pregnant or nursing.

2) Addition of foods concentrated in calories (dried fruits, nuts, seeds) to the basic diet of healthy individuals with unusually high caloric needs.

3) Elimination of foods that cause adverse reactions such as an allergy or an irritation.

4) Limitation of foods high in protein (legumes) to one cup a day for most people and further restriction in persons with certain illnesses (osteoporosis, gout, kidney stones, liver or kidney failure).

5) Fruits may have to be limited in those very sensitive to simple sugars (elevated triglycerides and hypoglycemia). In general three fruits a day is reasonable for most people.

6) One teaspoon of added salt over the surface of the foods is permitted in the daily diet of those who do not suffer from salt sensitive conditions (high blood pressure, heart or kidney disease and edema).

7) Children are solely breastfed until the age of six months, solid foods are then supplemented, but breast milk still constitutes 50-25% of the childs diet until age two. After this age starches, vegetables and fruits provide for the basic nutritional needs.

I

PERSONS WHO ARE ILL OR ON MEDICATION WHO WISH TO CHANGE THEIR DIET SHOULD DO SO ONLY UNDER THE DIRECTION OF A PHYSICIAN FAMILIAR WITH THE EFFECTS OF DIET ON HEALTH. Otherwise you are encouraged to start today this meal plan and lifestyle, which has provided excellent support for the health of most of our ancestors from the beginning of time and will do the same for you.

# INTRODUCTION

The appeal of foods comes from their richness of flavors, aromas, colors, and shapes. These pleasures to our senses are most abundant in the spices, starches, vegetables and fruits that make up the essential ingredients of *The McDougall Plan*. The wide variety to choose from provides boundless opportunities to create new and interesting recipes.

In this volume you will find many ideas for international dishes. Unusual spices and new twists on combinations of ingredients result in flavors that complement each other. This does not necessarily mean more kitchen time for you. The Quick and Easy section of this volume offers even more recipes than the previous books.

This volume is not simply another collection of recipes, but more importantly represents the personal development of my creative abilities. For more than 10 years I have been experimenting with ingredients and designing meals for my family and friends. In the beginning, you better believe, I had my share of disasters. But each year I've improved, and the products of my efforts show this progress.

Using ones talents to make someone else's life a little better has great rewards. I receive much pleasure from the contribution my work offers to you and your family. You will also find many recipes from others in this volume. Creative people are the important resource of new information that insures a wide variety of recipe ideas to meet almost everyones expectations for mouth watering meals. Please join me in my work by sending me your ideas so I can share them with others in future volumes. Everyone benefits. Write to me at

Mary McDougall
c/o P.O. Box 14039
Santa Rosa, CA 95402

# Recipes

Recipes with this symbol contain high-fat plant foods:

Recipes with this symbol contain foods with simple sugars:

Recipes with this symbol contain added salt
(soy sauce-tamari):

Recipes with this symbol contain high-protein foods
(Legumes):

In many recipes the simple sugars, salt, and high protein ingredients can be reduced or completely eliminated for people requiring more restricted diets.

# Breakfasts

## CASHEW FRENCH TOAST

SERVINGS: 16 slices

PREPARATION TIME: 10 mins.    COOKING TIME: 15 mins.

½ cup raw cashews
2¼ cup water
3 tbsp. chopped dates

⅛ tsp. cinnamon
dash turmeric
16 slices whole wheat bread

Place ingredients into a blender jar (except for the bread). Blend until smooth. Strain into a bowl. Dip slices of bread into mixture, coating both sides. Brown on a medium-hot, non-stick griddle, turning once so both sides are evenly browned. Serve plain, with fruit sauces or pure maple syrup.

HELPFUL HINTS: For a large amount, the recipe can easily be doubled. This freezes very nicely if individually wrapped and can be popped into the toaster for reheating.

## PAT'S FAVORITE PANCAKES

SERVINGS: 12 PANCAKES

PREPARATION TIME: 10 mins.    COOKING TIME: 20 mins.

1 cup whole wheat flour
1½ tsp. baking powder
1¼ cups acceptable milk or juice

1¼ cups applesauce (unsweetened)
½ tsp. vanilla
1 tsp. egg replacer, well mixed and
    beaten with 2 tbsp. water

Mix dry ingredients together (except the egg replacer). Mix wet ingredients together. Combine and beat until well blended. Pour batter onto hot non-stick griddle. When bubbles form on top and edges are beginning to dry out, turn to bake other side.

HELPFUL HINTS: These pancakes are wonderful with a little applesauce spread over them and sprinkled with cinnamon.

*Contributed by Don Henrud M.D.*

## RAWOLA

SERVINGS: 1

PREPARATION TIME: 5 mins.    COOKING TIME: none
(need cooked rice)

⅓ cup cooked cold brown rice          ⅓ cup Grapenuts
⅓ cup rolled oats

Combine above ingredients in a small bowl and mix well. Top with cinnamon, raisins and sliced bananas. Pour a little rice milk or apple juice over the mixture and enjoy it for breakfast.

*Contributed by Sharon Swindle*

## YEAST PANCAKES

SERVINGS: 8-10 pancakes

PREPARATION TIME: 10 mins.    COOKING TIME: 10 mins.
(needs time to rise)

1½ cups whole wheat flour          1 tbsp. active dry yeast
½ cup oatmeal                      1 ½ cups warm water

Mix dry ingredients together. Add the water. Mix. Allow to rise in a warm place until nearly double in volume (15-60 minutes). Cook on a non-stick griddle over medium heat. (Flatten the pancakes with the back of a spoon, if necessary.) Turn once when bubbles appear.

HELPFUL HINTS: This recipe can esily be varied by changing the types of flour and cereals used. Try adding mashed banana or applesauce to the batter. It adds an interesting flavor and the batter will rise faster.

## SCRAMBLED TOFU

SERVINGS: 4

PREPARATION TIME: 10 mins.    COOKING TIME: 10 mins.

1 small onion, chopped                1 tbsp. low sodium soy sauce
½ green pepper, chopped (optional)    ¼ to ½ tsp. turmeric
2 cups tofu, drained and crumbled     dash pepper

Saute onion and green pepper in ¼ cup water until soft. Add remaining ingredients. Cook and stir over medium heat about 5 minutes.

HELPFUL HINTS: This dish resembles scrambled eggs in color and texture. The vegetables used may be varied or eliminated entirely as you choose.

# Breads & Muffins

## PINEAPPLE MUFFINS

### SERVINGS: 15 muffins

PREPARATION TIME: 20 mins.   COOKING TIME: 15-20 mins.

2 cups whole wheat flour
¼ cup sunflower seeds
1 tbsp. baking powder
½ tsp. cinnamon
½ tsp. allspice

2 cups crushed pineapple in juice
¼ cup honey
2 tbsp. unsulphured molasses
2 tbsp. applesauce
1 tsp. egg replacer, well-mixed in 2 tbsp. water

Combine the dry ingredients together in a large bowl. Combine wet ingredients in a separate bowl. Add wet ingredients to dry ingredients. Stir to mix. Spoon into muffin cups (use non-stick pan, if possible). Fill cups only to about ¾ full. Bake at 375 degrees for 15-20 minutes.

HELPFUL HINTS: Do not use paper muffin cups—since there is no oil in these muffins, they will stick to the papers.

## *Contributed by Ed Quaintance*
## ED'S BREAD

### SERVINGS: 4 loaves

PREPARATION TIME: 1 hr.   COOKING TIME: 40 mins.
RISING TIME: 1 hr.

4 cups warm water
½ lb. raisins
11 oz. "hi gluten" flour

3 lb. 5 oz. whole wheat flour
3 pkg. rapid rise yeast (¼ oz pkg.)

Place the raisins in a little of the water to plump them up. Then puree in blender until smooth. Mix all of the above ingredients together. Stir until well mixed. Begin to knead when no longer able to stir. Knead in bowl until dough does not stick to sides. Turn out on to a floured board. Knead until dough has a satiny consistency, adding flour as necessary to prevent sticking.

(This will take about 12 mins.) Return to bowl, cover and let rise until doubled in size, about 30 minutes at room temperature. Pat out flat, fold into thirds, pat flat again, fold into thirds the opposite way. Slice into 4 pieces (approximately 1 lb, 10 oz each). Place in silicon coated pans (Baker's Secret) or lightly oiled pans without further kneading or forming of the loaf. Let rise 30 minutes more or until doubled in size. Bake at 325 degrees for 40 mins. Remove from pans, cool on rack.

HELPFUL HINTS: If you have a large Kitchenaid mixer then the mixing and kneading can all be done in the same bowl by this mixer. A real time and work saver!

## OATMEAL MUFFINS

SERVINGS: makes about 16 muffins

PREPARATION TIME: 30 mins.     COOKING TIME: 15-20 mins.

1¼ cups whole wheat flour
⅔ cup quick cooking rolled oats
4 tbsp. bran
2 tsp. baking powder
½ tsp. baking soda
½ cup honey

½ cup peanut butter
2 tsp. egg replacer-well mixed
with 4 tbsp. of water
1 cup nut, soy or rice milk
1 cup raisins or chopped dates

Stir the flour, oats, bran, baking powder, and baking soda together. Beat peanut butter and honey together (use medium speed on a mixer if you have one). Add egg replacer mixture and beat well. Add the flour mixture and the milk alternately to the beaten mixture, beating on low speed just until blended. Stir in raisins or dates. Spoon into muffin cups (use non-stick pan or very lightly oiled muffin tins.) Do not use paper muffin cups—they stick! Fill each about ¾ full. Bake at 400 degrees for 15-20 minutes.

## CROUTONS

SERVINGS: variable

PREPARATION TIME: 5 mins.     COOKING TIME: 5 mins.

whole wheat bread slices

Remove the crusts from the bread. Cut each slice into squares. Place squares on a baking sheet and toast under broiler until lightly browned. Watch them carefully so they don't burn. Turn over to toast other side.

HELPFUL HINTS: The bread may be sprinkled with various seasonings before toasting. if desired. Try chili powder, curry powder, poultry seasoning or other of your favorites.

*Contributed by Patty*

## SPROUTED BREAD

SERVINGS: makes 1 baking sheet full

PREPARATION TIME: variable    COOKING TIME: 12 hrs.

1 cup wheat berries or other whole      ¼ cup sesame seeds
   grains
¾ cup sunflower seeds

(1) Sprout grain and seeds. Soak seeds 8 hours, drain, rinse and sprout for 2 days. Makes 2 cups sprouted seeds. Soak grains 12 hours, drain, rinse and sprout 2 days. Makes 3 cups sprouted grains.

(2) Grind sprouted seeds and grains together. Use blender, food processor or food mill. Add a little water if necessary.

(3) Add seasonings and mix thoroughly (see other suggestions under HELPFUL HINTS).

2 tbsp. low sodium soy sauce            1 tsp. parsley flakes
1 tsp. Vegit or other vegetable         1 tsp. dried minced onions
   seasonings.
⅛ tsp. garlic powder

(4) Spread on lightly oiled foil on a baking sheet about ⅛ inch thick. Dry out in oven overnight at lowest temperature. Turn over and peel off foil to dry the other side. Break in pieces. Store in air tight container.

HELPFUL HINTS: Other seasonings to try include:
Mexican: chili powder, chopped green chilies

Italian: basil, oregano, tomato sauce

Sweet: raisins or other dried fruit, cinnamon, nutmeg, mace, applesauce.

Score bread with a knife before baking to have even squares for serving.

# CHAPATIES

SERVINGS: makes about 12

PREPARATION TIME: 15 mins.    COOKING TIME: 4-5 min.
RESTING TIME: 45 min.

2 cups whole wheat flour              ⅔ to ¾ cups warm water

Mix flour and water together (start with ⅔ cup). Knead with your hands until it holds together, adding more water as necessary. Turn on to a floured board and knead for about 10 minutes. Shape into a ball and place in a bowl. Cover with a damp towel and let rest for 45 minutes. Divide dough into 12 equal portions. Roll out one at a time on a lightly floured board, until they are about 6 inches in diameter. Stack circles between sheets of waxed paper. Cook on a non-stick griddle or frying pan until top changes color. Press down with spatula. When bottom is lightly browned, about 2 to 2½ minutes, turn over and cook until the other side is browned. Serve hot.

*Contributed by Elaine French*
## ELAINE'S BRAN MUFFINS

SERVINGS: 12 muffins

PREPARATION TIME: 20 mins.    COOKING TIME: 20 mins.

1¼ cups whole wheat pastry flour    1 cup nut milk
1½ tsp. baking soda                 ¼ cup applesauce
1 tsp. egg replacer                 ¼ cup honey
1½ cups bran                        1 tsp. vanilla
5 oz. boiling water                 ½ cup raisins

Combine flour, soda and egg replacer. In a large bowl, pour boiling water over bran. Mix well. Add nut milk, applesauce, honey, vanilla and raisins. Blend well. Stir dry ingredients quickly into wet ingredients. Spoon batter into non stick muffin tin. Bake at 425 degrees for 20 minutes.

# Dressings, Dips & Spreads

*Contributed by Sherrie's White Flower Inn*
## SHERRIE'S OIL-FREE DRESSING

SERVINGS: makes 1 qt.

PREPARATION TIME: 10 mins.    COOKING TIME: none
(cooked beans needed)

1 ½ cups cooked garbanzo beans
2½ cups canned tomatoes

2 tbsp. lemon juice
½ tsp. dry basil

Place all ingredients in a blender. Process until just combined, not until perfectly smooth.

## VINAIGRETTE DRESSING

SERVINGS: makes 1½ cups

PREPARATION TIME: 10 mins.    COOKING TIME: none

1 cup unsweetened grapefruit juice
⅓ cup vinegar
4 tbsp. water
2 cloves garlic, crushed

½ tsp. basil
¼ tsp. thyme
1 tsp. chopped fresh parsley
freshly ground pepper

Place all ingredients in a jar with a tight fitting lid. Shake until well mixed. Keeps well in refrigerator.

## AVOCADO SALSA

SERVINGS: variable

PREPARATION TIME: 10 mins.    COOKING TIME: none

1 ripe avocado
3 tbsp. chopped fresh coriander
⅓ to ½ cup water

¾ tsp. Tabasco
½ tsp. vinegar
1 tsp. low sodium soy sauce

Peel and pit avocado. Coarsely chop and place in blender jar. Add remaining ingredients and blend until smooth.

HELPFUL HINTS: Use as a dip for vegetables or crackers. Or try as a topping for various foods, such as rice casserole, stuffed vegetables, or chapati roll-ups.

*Contributed by Milton DuPuy*
## TOFU SALAD DRESSING

SERVINGS: makes 2 cups

PREPARATION TIME: 10 mins.    COOKING TIME: none

½ onion, peeled & cut in chunks
1 tub tofu (16 oz.)
1-2 tsp. paprika

½ tsp. celery seed
several dashes garlic powder

Place onion and crumbled tofu in blender jar. Process until smooth, adding some water if necessary. Add remaining ingredients and process until well combined. Makes an excellent dressing for potato salad.

## HOT PEANUT DIP

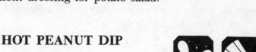

SERVINGS: makes 1 cup

PREPARATION TIME: 15 mins.    COOKING TIME: none

½ cup peanut butter
¼ cup low sodium soy sauce
2 tbsp. hot water
1 tbsp. lemon juice

1 tsp honey
1 clove garlic
½ to 1 tsp. dried red pepper flakes

Combine all ingredients in a blender and process using on/off method. Add a little more water if necessary to make a smooth dipping sauce. Serve at room temperature as a dip for assorted raw vegetables.

## TOMATO RELISH

SERVINGS: makes 2½ cups

PREPARATION TIME: 15 mins.    COOKING TIME: 25 mins.

2 medium onions, sliced
2 cloves garlic, minced or crushed
1 tsp. ground ginger
½ tsp. chili powder

¼ tsp. mustard seeds
¼ tsp. cumin seeds
15-16 oz. can tomatoes, chopped

Place onions, garlic, ginger, chili powder, mustard seeds and cumin seeds in a small amount of water and cook and stir for 3 minutes. Add tomatoes and cook, covered, over medium heat for 10 minutes. Then reduce heat and cook for an additional 10 minutes. Serve either hot or cold, as a side dish or on toast as a spread.

## SALSA CRUDA

SERVINGS: makes about 2½ cups

PREPARATION TIME: 15 min.    COOKING TIME: none

3 tomatoes, finely chopped or 1
  can (14 oz) tomatoes, finely
  chopped
1 medium onion, finely chopped

⅛ cup finely chopped jalapeno
  chilies
¼ cup chopped fresh coriander
¼ cup chopped green chilies

Combine all ingredients and mix well. Serve at room temperature. Serve on burritos or tostadas, with chips, or fresh vegetables.

HELPFUL HINTS: May also be processed briefly in a blender.

## DIJON TOFU DIP

SERVINGS: 2½ cups

PREPARATION TIME: 10 mins.   COOKING TIME: none

16-20 oz. tub of tofu, drained
2 tbsp. low sodium soy sauce
4 tsp. Dijon mustard
½ tsp. horseradish powder or 2
   tsp. pure prepared horseradish

1 tsp. dill weed
½ tsp. onion powder
2 cloves garlic, pressed
4 tbsp. chopped fresh coriander
   leaves

Combine all ingredients in a blender or food processor. Process until smooth. Add a little water if necessary for ease in preparation.

HELPFUL HINTS: This makes quite a large amount of dip. It keeps well in the refrigerator. Makes a delicious topping for baked potatoes.

## ONION SOUP DIP

SERVINGS: makes 2 cups

PREPARATION TIME: 5 min. CHILLING TIME: 2 hrs.

1 lb. tub tofu
½ cup water
1 tbsp. lemon juice

1 pkg. natural dehydrated onion
   soup mix
(example: Hain)

Crumble tofu and place in blender jar with water and lemon juice. Process until very smooth. Transfer to a bowl. Stir in onion soup mix. Cover and chill for at least 2 hrs. for flavors to blend.

Serve with raw vegetables or crackers, pita bread, breadsticks, and other whole grain products. Also good as a topping for baked potatoes.

## DILLY TOFU DIP

SERVINGS: makes 2 cups

PREPARATION TIME: 10 mins.   COOKING TIME: none

1 lb tub tofu
1 tbsp. low sodium soy sauce
1 tbsp. natural Worcestershire
  Sauce
1 tbsp. lemon juice

2½ tsp. parsley flakes
2½ tsp. dill weed
dash or two of white pepper

Drain the tofu and crumble it into a blender jar. Process until smooth, adding a little water if necessary to make blending easier. Add remaining ingredients and process until well blended. Refrigerate until serving time.

HELPFUL HINTS: Chilling before serving is recommended to allow time for flavors to blend.

## WHITE BEAN SPREAD

SERVINGS: makes 1½ cups

PREPARATION TIME: 15 mins.       COOKING TIME: 20 mins.
  (cooked beans needed)          CHILLING TIME: 2 hrs.

1 small onion, finely chopped
1 clove garlic, pressed
2 tbsp. chopped green chilies
⅛ tsp. cayenne pepper

2 cups cooked white beans
1 tbsp. low sodium soy sauce
2 tbsp. sherry (or apple juice)

Place onion, garlic, and green chilies in a sauce pan with a small amount of water. Cook and stir until onion is very soft. Add cayenne pepper and mix in well. Add beans, cook, mashing them with either a bean masher or a fork as they cook. Add soy sauce and sherry. Cook and stir for several minutes. Transfer to a bowl. Cover and refrigerate for at least 2 hours.

Use as a spread for crackers, or a dip for pita, or as a sandwich spread.

### *Contributed by Elaine French*
## HUMMUS

SERVINGS: makes about 2 cups

PREPARATION TIME: 10 mins.     COOKING TIME: none
          (cooked beans needed)

1 cup cooked garbanzos
½ cup tahini
⅓ cup lemon juice

½ cup bean liquid or water
2 cloves garlic, cut in small pieces

**IN FOOD PROCESSOR:**

Mix garbanzos, tahini and garlic. Scrape sides once to make sure ingredients are well mixed. With machine running, add lemon juice and bean liquid through feeder tube. Mix until smooth.

**IN BLENDER:**

Combine all ingredients, except garbanzos and blend until smooth. With machine running, add garbanzos a few at a time until mixture is thick.

Serve as a dip with whole wheat pita bread or with raw vegetables. Also makes a delicious sandwich spread.

## KIDNEY BEAN SPREAD

SERVINGS: makes 1¼ cups

PREPARATION TIME: 5 mins.    COOKING TIME: none
(cooked beans needed)

1½ cups cooked kidney beans
1 clove garlic
½ tsp. cumin seeds
½ tsp. Tabasco sauce

½ tbsp. vinegar
2 tbsp. water
2 tbsp. fresh coriander leaves

Place all ingredients in a food processor or blender and process until smooth.

HELPFUL HINTS: Makes a delicious sandwich spread or dip for crackers.

*Contributed by Helen Rubin*

## SPICY BEAN SPREAD

SERVINGS: makes about 3 cups

PREPARATION TIME: 15 mins.    COOKING TIME: none
(cooked beans needed)

4 cups cooked beans (kidney, pinto, or red)
1 onion, chopped
3-4 tomatoes, chopped
2 cloves garlic
2 tbsp. low sodium soy sauce

1 tbsp. chili powder
1 tbsp. ground cumin
1 tsp. paprika
1 tsp. oregano

Place all ingredients in a food processor, blender or food mill. Process until smooth. Use as a sandwich spread or as a dip for pita or raw vegetables.

HELPFUL HINTS: A little water may be added if necessary during processing. This is quite highly spiced, too much so for some people. Reduce the amount of spices in half if you like less spicy foods.

## SPICY BEAN SPREAD II

SERVINGS: makes 4 ½ cups

PREPARATION TIME: 45 mins.     COOKING TIME: 30 mins.
(cooked beans needed)

| | |
|---|---|
| 1-2 cups bean cooking liquid | 1 tbsp. chili powder |
| 5 cups cooked pinto beans | 1 tsp. ground cumin |
| 1 onion, finely chopped | ½ tsp. oregano |
| 1 clove garlic, crushed | Tabasco sauce to taste |

In a large pot, place the onions and garlic in a small amount of water and cook and stir until onion is soft. Add a small amount of beans, some bean liquid and mash into the onion and garlic. Repeat until all the beans are mashed and smooth. Add Chili powder, cumin, oregano and Tabasco sauce to taste. Cook and stir until bean mixture thickens, about 15 minutes. In a food processor or blender, process bean mixture until smooth.

HELPFUL HINTS: Water may be used in place of the bean cooking liquid. Use as a spread for crackers, pita or sandwiches.

# Appetizers

## MARINATED MUSHROOMS

SERVINGS: variable

PREPARATION TIME: 15 mins. CHILLING TIME: 2-3 hrs.

| | |
|---|---|
| 1 lb. bite-sized mushrooms | 1 cup water |
| 2 green peppers, cut into ¾ inch pieces | 1 tbsp. honey |
| | 2 tsp. dry mustard |
| 1 small onion, cut into wedges and then separated | 2 tsp. low sodium soy sauce |
| 1 cup red wine vinegar | |

Prepare mushrooms by cleaning and trimming stems. Set aside with green pepper and onions in a bowl. Combine water, vinegar, honey, mustard and soy sauce in a pan. Bring to a boil. Pour over mushrooms, green peppers and onions. Cover. Marinate in refrigerator for several hours.

Before serving, thread on small bamboo skewers. Serve as an appetizer.

# SUSHI

SERVINGS: 8-10 sushi rolls
(each roll cuts into 8 pieces)

PREPARATION TIME: 1½ hrs.    COOKING TIME: none
(hot cooked rice needed)

8-10 sheets nori seaweed
10 cups hot cooked short grain
  brown rice
¾ cup rice vinegar
4 tbsp. honey

2-3 carrots, grated
2 bunches green onions, finely
  chopped
1 cucumber, peeled, pitted, finely
  chopped
½ bunch parsley, minced

Place the hot cooked rice in a large oblong baking dish. Pour the vinegar and honey over the rice, add a dash or two of soy sauce if desired. Stir with a flat spatula or rice paddle. Fan rice to cool rapidly while stirring constantly. (Use an electric fan or a hand fan.) The rice must be cooled quickly so it will be glossy and lightly dry.

Steam the vegetables over boiling water for 5 minutes. Mix into the vine-gared rice.

Toast the nori sheets by passing 1 side of the seaweed over a hot burner for 5-10 seconds.

Place the nori on a bamboo mat (maki-su) or on a kitchen towel. Spread about 1 cup of the rice mixture evenly on the nori. Press against the seaweed well. Keep your hands wet to prevent the rice from sticking to them. Place filling 2 inches from the side nearest to you. Start to roll the sushi from the end closest to you. Use the bamboo mat or towel to help you roll the sushi. Keep pressure on the roll at all times. When you get to the end of the nori, moisten the edge with a little water to seal the nori around the rice. Squeeze the sushi tightly to form a compact roll. (This will probably take a little practice. Each time you make one it will be easier!) Set the sushi roll aside, seam side down on a sheet of waxed paper. Wait for 15 minutes before slicing. May be chilled before slicing. May also be stored unsliced, wrapped in waxed paper, in the refrigerator for several days.

To slice, use a very sharp knife (not serrated.) Moisten knife blade before each cut. Cut the sushi "log" in half, then into fourths, then into eighths.

Sushi will keep at room temperature for 6-8 hours.

Serve with soy sauce for dipping, or try dipping them in Oriental Dipping Sauce. May also be eaten plain.

HELPFUL HINTS: This takes quite a bit of time to prepare, but it makes a lot of sushi. It is an excellent appetizer for a party. It is also ideal to take along to a picnic or a potluck dinner.

The vegetables listed are only suggestions. Use any vegetable you prefer, just keep the pieces small.

Traditional sushi is usually made with the strips of vegetables placed in the center of the vinegared rice. I prefer to make them this way, both for flavor and convenience. If you would like to make them with the vegetables in the center, do not mix the vegetables into the vinegared rice. Instead slice into thin strips some carrots, cucumbers, radishes, bamboo shoots, etc. Steam for about 5 minutes. After spreading the rice on the nori, arrange some of these vegetables down the center of the rice. Roll as directed above.

*Contributed by Elaine French*

### LENTIL-MUSHROOM PATE

SERVINGS: makes about 4 cups

PREPARATION TIME: 15 mins.    COOKING TIME: 50 mins.

| | |
|---|---|
| 1 cup lentils | 1 tsp. sage |
| 4 cups water | 1 tsp. thyme |
| ½ lb. mushrooms, sliced | 1 tsp. dry mustard |
| 1 onion, chopped | ½ tsp. cayenne pepper |
| 1 clove garlic, crushed | ¼ tsp. black pepper |
| 1 tbsp. parsley flakes | ¼ tsp. allspice |
| 1 tsp. basil | ¼ tsp. ground ginger |
| 1 tsp. chervil | 1 bay leaf |
| 1 tsp. marjoram | 2 tbsp. low sodium soy sauce |
| 1 tsp. rosemary | 1 tbsp. sherry |

Cook lentils in the water until tender (about 40 minutes), and drain them in a strainer. While lentils are cooking, saute onion and garlic in ¼ cup water over medium heat for 5 minutes. Add mushrooms and saute 5 minutes longer. Add herbs and spices and continue to cook for 10 more minutes, adding more water as needed. Add soy sauce, sherry, and drained lentils. Cook until liquid is absorbed and mixture starts to stick to pan. Take from heat, remove bay leaf, and puree mixture in food processor or blender until smooth. Serve warm or chilled.

HELPFUL HINTS: Serve as an appetizer with triangles of whole wheat toast. Also good spread on thin, crisp, rye crackers.

# STUFFED MUSHROOM CAPS

SERVINGS: variable

PREPARATION TIME: 40 mins.    COOKING TIME: 15 mins.

38-40 medium-large mushrooms
  (20-22 extra large size)
1 (10 oz.) pkg.frozen chopped
  spinach
1 pkg. dehydrated onion soup mix
  (such as Hain)

1½ cups soft blended tofu
½ tsp. garlic powder (optional)

Thaw spinach and press out liquid. Clean mushrooms, remove stems and arrange on non-stick baking sheet, stem side up. Combine soup mix, tofu, garlic powder and thawed spinach. Mix well.

Place a small amount of the spinach mixture into each mushroom cap and flatten slightly. Repeat until all are filled. Cover. Bake, covered, in a 350 degrees oven for 15 minutes.

Serve hot as an appetizer.

HELPFUL HINTS: This may be made ahead of time. Refrigerate until baking time.

If you can't find large mushrooms, use medium ones. You will need to buy a few more in that case.

There are many "natural" onion soup mixes on the market. Look for ones that do not contain oil.

This is also delicious made with Tofu Mayonnaise or Dijon Tofu Dip instead of the plain blended tofu.

Check after cooking for 12 minutes. Sometimes smaller mushrooms cook faster.

# ROASTED LEGUMES

SERVINGS: variable

PREPARATION TIME: 15-30 mins.    COOKING TIME: 30-45 mins.

1 cup dry legumes (garbanzo
  beans, lentils, red lentils, split
  peas)

Place the legume of your choice (except red lentils) in a sauce pan with 1 quart of water. Bring to a boil. Cover and remove from heat. Let stand until tender enough to chew (15-30 minutes for garbanzos and lentils, 10 minutes for the split peas). To prepare red lentils, put in a bowl and cover with hot water. Let stand until tender, about 10 minutes.

Drain well. Place on a non-stick baking sheet. Sprinkle with seasonings of your choice (suggestions follow). Bake in a 350 degree oven until dry and toasted, 30 to 45 minutes. Approximate baking times: Red Lentils about 30 minutes
Lentils and split peas about 35 minutes
Garbanzos about 45 minutes

Loosen with a spatula after 15 minutes, then shake occasionally while baking.

Store in an airtight container for a delicious snack food.

HELPFUL HINTS: Some suggested seasonings:
Chili powder and paprika
Curry powder
Cumin and garlic powder
Onion powder and garlic powder

# POPCORN

SERVINGS: variable

PREPARATION TIME: 5 mins.    COOKING TIME: 5 mins.

Popcorn

Use an air popper, no oil is necessary for popping. A special popper can also be purchased for a microwave oven that requires no oil.

For seasoning use some low-sodium soy sauce. Place in a small spray bottle and lightly spray over the popcorn while gently shaking. The spray bottle technique can also be used with plain water to moisten the popcorn before shaking on your favorite seasoning to help the seasoning stick to the surface. Try chili powder, poultry seasoning, curry powder, onion powder or paprika.

## CAJUN SPICES

SERVINGS: makes ⅓ cup

PREPARATION TIME: 5 mins.    COOKING TIME: none

3 tbsp. paprika
2 tsp. onion powder
2 tsp. ground black pepper
2 tsp. ground white pepper

2 tsp. ground red pepper
1 tsp. oregano
1 tsp. thyme
½ tsp. celery seed

Mix all ingredients and store in a tightly covered container.

HELPFUL HINTS: Makes an excellent spicy topping for popcorn. Try adding some of this to the New Orleans Creole Sauce ( recipe in this volume). Spices may be irritating to some sensitive people.

# Sauces

### *Contributed by Marilyn Meyers*

## SPICY MEXICAN TOMATO SAUCE

SERVINGS: makes 1½ cups

PREPARATION TIME: 5 mins.    COOKING TIME: 10 mins.

1 (15 oz.) can tomato sauce
2 cloves garlic, pressed
1½ tsp. chili powder

½ tsp. oregano leaves
½ tsp. ground cumin

Place all ingredients in a saucepan and simmer uncovered for 10 minutes.

HELPFUL HINTS: Use this sauce to make Mexican Pizza, as follows:
Step 1: Oven crisped tortilla, soft chapati or soft pita
Step 2: Spread with "refried" beans
Step 3: Spread with Spicy Mexican Tomato Sauce
Step 4: Top with diced green chilies, chopped onion, chopped black olives, etc.
Step 5: Bake at 350 degrees until beans are hot (just a few minutes) garnish with chopped lettuce, radishes, and sprouts.

# CREAMY MUSHROOM SAUCE

SERVINGS: makes about 3 cups

PREPARATION TIME: 15 mins.    COOKING TIME: 25 mins.

1 onion, chopped
½ lb. mushrooms, sliced
2 cups nut milk, soy milk or rice
  milk
1 tbsp. low sodium soy sauce

⅛ tsp. white pepper
⅛ tsp. garlic powder
2 tbsp. cornstarch or arrowroot

Saute the mushrooms and onions in ¼ cup water for 10 minutes. Add acceptable milk, soy sauce, garlic powder and white pepper. Mix cornstarch or arrowroot in ¼ cup cold water. Add to mushroom mixture. Cook and stir over medium heat until mixture thickens.

Serve over potatoes, vegetables, grains, etc. An excellent topping for the potato-veggie dinner (recipe in this book).

# SWEET AND SOUR FRUIT SAUCE

SERVINGS: 1½ Cups

PREPARATION TIME: 15 mins.    COOKING TIME: 30 mins.

2 cups apples and pears, peeled
  and chopped
⅓ cup water
2 tbsp. cider vinegar

3 tbsp. honey
1 tsp. low sodium soy sauce

Combine all ingredients in a saucepan. Cover and cook until fruit is tender, about 30 minutes. Mash with a hand masher. Serve warm or cold.

### *Contributed by Milton DuPuy*
# MILTON'S BARBEQUE SAUCE

SERVINGS: makes 2 cups

PREPARATION TIME: 10 mins.    COOKING TIME: none

1 (15-16 oz.) can tomato sauce
1 to 1½ tbsp. molasses
1 tbsp. prepared mustard
1 to 1½ tbsp. honey

½ tsp. onion powder
⅛ tsp. allspice
⅛ tsp. nutmeg
⅛ tsp. cayenne

Combine all ingredients. Use in any recipe calling for barbeque sauce.

# DILL SAUCE

SERVINGS: makes 2½ cups

PREPARATION TIME: 5 mins.    COOKING TIME: 10 mins.

2 tbsp. cornstarch or arrowroot
3 tbsp. water
1 ½ tsp. dried dill weed
2 cups nut milk
¼ cup white wine (or white grape juice)

1 tsp. lemon juice
½ tsp. honey
⅛ tsp. nutmeg
dash or two of white pepper

Mix cornstarch and water in a saucepan. Add dill weed, milk and wine (or juice). Cook and stir over medium heat until sauce thickens and is smooth. Add remaining ingredients. Cook and stir for a couple of minutes. Serve hot.

HELPFUL HINTS: This is excellent served over broccoli, Brussels sprouts, cauliflower or stuffed vegetables.

# TAHINI SAUCE

SERVINGS: makes 2 cups

PREPARATION TIME: 5 mins.    COOKING TIME: none

1 cup sesame tahini
¾ cup water

¼ cup lemon juice
1 or 2 cloves garlic

Combine all ingredients in a blender jar. Blend until smooth. Serve as a dip, spread on crackers or bread, or with falafels. This is a rich sauce because sesame seeds, from which tahini is made, are high in fat.

# ORIENTAL DIPPING SAUCE

SERVINGS: 2

PREPARATION TIME: 5 mins.    COOKING TIME: none

¼ cup. low sodium soy sauce
½ tsp. Japanese horseradish
   powder or Eutrema mustard or
   Chinese hot mustard
1 tbsp. water

Mix horseradish or mustard with the water. Stir until smooth. Add soy sauce. Serve as a dipping sauce for sushi or Spring rolls.

HELPFUL HINTS: This is quite salty and should be used infrequently. It also can be quite spicy. Reduce the amount of mustard or horseradish for a less spicy version.

## PINEAPPLE SWEET AND SOUR SAUCE

SERVINGS: makes 3 ½ cups

PREPARATION TIME: 10 mins.     COOKING TIME: 10-15 mins.

1 (20 oz.) can crushed pineapple
   and unsweetened juice
½ cup cider vinegar
½ cup honey
3 tbsp. low sodium soy sauce
2 tbsp. cornstarch or arrowroot

Place pineapple and its juice in a blender jar. Process until smooth.

Place all ingredients in a saucepan. Cook and stir over medium heat until thickenened.

## APRICOT CHUTNEY SAUCE

SERVINGS: makes 4 ½ cups

PREPARATION TIME: 15 mins.     COOKING TIME: 45 mins.

¾ cup chopped dried apricots
3 cups water
1 ¼ cups mango chutney
¼ cup vinegar
1 tbsp. grated fresh ginger root

½ tsp. dry mustard
2 tbsp. honey
2½ cups water
2 tbsp. cornstarch or arrowroot

Cook the apricots in 3 cups water until very soft. Mash them with a fork as much as possible. Most of the water should be absorbed by this time. Add the remaining ingredients. Cook and stir until thickened.

Serve as a sauce over filled chapatis, as a condiment with curried foods, or as a sweet and sour sauce.

## ALMOND SAUCE

SERVINGS: makes 2½ cups

PREPARATION TIME: 5 mins.     COOKING TIME: 10-15 mins.

½ cup almonds
2¾ cups water
2 tbsp. low sodium soy sauce
1 clove garlic, pressed

¼ tsp. turmeric
dash or two white pepper
2½ tbsp. cornstarch or arrowroot

Place almonds and water in blender jar. Process until smooth. Strain into saucepan. Add remaining ingredients. Cook and stir over medium high heat until thickened.

HELPFUL HINTS: Serve over stuffed vegetables, chapati rolls, grain casseroles, or anything that sounds good to you.

# Soups

## FRENCH VEGETABLE SOUP

### SERVINGS: 8-10

PREPARATION TIME: 30 mins.    COOKING TIME: 45 mins.

8 cups water
2 onions, coarsely chopped
1 clove garlic, crushed
2 potatoes, chopped coarsely
1 stalk celery, thickly sliced
1 carrot, thickly sliced
½ lb. mushrooms, sliced
4 zucchini, thickly sliced (cut in half)
2 leeks, sliced
  or 1 bunch green onions, sliced

2 cups chopped broccoli pieces
1 cup fresh or frozen peas
1 cup chopped cauliflower pieces
1 cup dry white wine
1 tsp. thyme
1 tsp. dill weed
1 tsp. marjoram
1 tsp. basil
3 tbsp. low sodium soy sauce
fresh, ground black pepper

Place 8 cups water in a large soup pot. Add onions, potatoes, garlic, celery and carrots. Bring to a boil, reduce heat, cover, and simmer for 15 minutes. Add remaining ingredients, cook an additional 30 minutes.

Sprinkle with finely chopped green onions before serving, if desired.

## KOMBU STOCK
## (JAPANESE SOUP STOCK)

### SERVINGS: 4 cups

PREPARATION TIME: 5 mins.    COOKING TIME: 5 mins.

6 inches Kombu

4 cups water

(Kombu is a seaweed.) Wash Kombu under running water to remove excess salt. Place in sauce pan with water. Bring to boil. Cover and cook about 2-3 minutes. Remove Kombu and discard. Use stock as a soup base or in other recipes.

*Contributed by Paul E. Hunter*

## HUNTER'S FLAT BEAN SOUP

SERVINGS: 10-12

PREPARATION TIME: 20 mins.    COOKING TIME: 2½ hrs.

| | |
|---|---|
| 10 cups water | 1 green chili pepper, chopped |
| ¾ cup lentils | (canned) |
| 1¼ cups lima beans | 2 cups shredded cabbage |
| 2 carrots, chopped | 1 (28 oz.) can tomatoes, chopped |
| 2 stalks celery, chopped | 1 tsp. garlic powder |
| 2 onions, chopped | 1 tbsp. low sodium soy sauce |

Place legumes in a large pot with the water. Bring to a boil, cover, reduce heat to medium-low and cook for 1 hour. Add carrots, celery, onions, chili pepper, tomatoes and seasonings. Cook for an additional hour. Add cabbage and simmer for 30 minutes longer.

HELPFUL HINTS: If soup gets too thick, add more water while cooking.

*Contributed by Paul E. Hunter*

## SPICY PEA SOUP

SERVINGS: 10-12

PREPARATION TIME: 15 mins.    COOKING TIME: 2 hrs.

| | |
|---|---|
| 10 cups water | 1 tsp. onion powder |
| 1½ cups split green peas | 1 tsp. garlic powder |
| 2 carrots, finely diced | 1 tsp. paprika |
| 2 stalks celery, finely diced | ¼ tsp. cayenne |
| 1 large onion, finely chopped | 2 tbsp. low sodium soy sauce |

Place peas and water in a large pot. Bring to a boil, reduce heat to medium low, add remaining ingredients, cover and cook for 2 hours. Stir occasionally. When the ingredients are smooth like a puree, serve.

HELPFUL HINTS: Stirring with a wisk helps to blend the ingredients.

*Contributed by Ruth Heidrich*
## SOUP IN A PUMPKIN

SERVINGS: variable

PREPARATION TIME: variable     COOKING TIME: 1½ hrs.

1 (6-7 lb.) pumpkin
6-8 cups hot soup

Cut a round cover out of the pumpkin top (as if you were making a jack-o-lantern). Scrape out the seeds and stringy portion. Fill with soup mixture. Place cover on top.

Bake in a baking pan in a 400 degree oven for about 1½ hours. Cook only until softened; if overcooked, pumpkin will collapse. If you need to keep it warm until serving time, lower heat to 175 degrees.

HELPFUL HINTS: Most any soup will do, although thick soups are preferable. If soup is thin, add 2-3 cups of dried whole wheat bread crumbs or chunks. When serving, ladle soup into bowls, scraping off some of the flesh from inside the pumpkin.

## FRENCH PEASANT SOUP

SERVINGS: 6-8

PREPARATION TIME: 20 mins.     COOKING TIME: 1½ hrs.

8 cups water
1 cup dried lima beans
½ cup dried yellow split peas
1 cup bulgur wheat
1 large onion, chopped
2 cloves garlic, crushed
3 cups chopped cabbage
3 cups winter squash, peeled and chopped
2 potatoes, chopped

1 (16 oz) can tomatoes, chopped
3 tbsp. low sodium soy sauce
⅛ tsp. crushed red pepper
½ tsp. tarragon
½ tsp. chervil
¼ tsp. marjoram
¼ tsp. thyme
1 tbsp. parsley flakes

Place water in a large soup pot. Add lima beans and cook over medium heat for 30 minutes. Add remaining ingredients. Cook an additional 60 minutes.

HELPFUL HINTS: This is a simple peasant soup. It may also be served over potatoes, stuffed in pita bread or rolled up in chapati. It makes a good sandwich spread when cold.

# CURRIED PUMPKIN SOUP

### SERVINGS: 4-6

PREPARATION TIME: 20 mins.     COOKING TIME: 30 mins.

1 onion, chopped
½ lb. mushrooms, sliced
2 tbsp. whole wheat flour
1 tbsp. curry powder
3 cups water
1 (16 oz.) can pumpkin puree

1 tbsp. honey
1 tbsp. low sodium soy sauce
dash of ground nutmeg
1 cup nut milk (recipe in The
   McDougall Plan) or soy milk

Place the onion and mushrooms in a large soup pot with a small amount of water. Cook over medium heat for 3-4 minutes. Add the flour and curry powder. Cook and stir over low heat to brown flour for about 3 minutes. Slowly add the water while stirring (use a whisk if you have one), then add the pumpkin, honey, soy sauce, and nutmeg. Simmer over low heat, stirring occasionally, about 15 minutes. Stir in the nut or soy milk, heat thoroughly, but do not boil. Serve at once.

*Contributed by Linda and Milton DuPuy*

# FRESH VEGETABLE SOUP

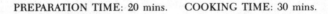

### SERVINGS: 4

PREPARATION TIME: 20 mins.     COOKING TIME: 30 mins.

4 cups water
2 medium potatoes, chopped
2 medium carrots, sliced
1 medium zucchini, halved
   lengthwise, then sliced
1 large onion, chopped

1 cup chopped celery leaves
2 ribs celery, sliced
½ to 1 tsp. herb seasoning blend
2 tbsp. low sodium soy sauce
2 cups thin strips fresh spinach
½ tsp. fresh ground pepper

Combine all ingredients except spinach and pepper in a large pot. Bring to a boil, reduce heat, cover and simmer 15-20 minutes, or until potatoes and carrots are tender. Add spinach, cover and cook 2 minutes. Season with pepper before serving.

*Contributed by Milton and Linda DuPuy*

# CHRISTMAS EVE SOUP

### SERVINGS: 6

PREPARATION TIME: 30 mins.     COOKING TIME: 45 mins.

1 large onion, chopped
2 cups chopped cauliflower
2 cups chopped broccoli
1 cup chopped carrots
1 cup chopped celery
2 cups chopped spinach
2 (28 oz.) cans tomatoes, blended
1 cup water
1 tbsp. parsley
2 tbsp. low sodium soy sauce

¼ tsp. each: cumin
celery seed
basil
rosemary
curry powder
dill weed
paprika
cayenne pepper
dash of ground ginger
dash of black pepper

Place all ingredients in a large soup pot. Bring to a boil, reduce heat, cover and cook over medium heat until vegetables are tender.

# COLOMBIAN DINNER SOUP

## SERVINGS: 4-6

PREPARATION TIME: 45 mins.    COOKING TIME: 1 hr.

1 qt. water
1 lb. boiling onions, cleaned and
   left whole
1 clove garlic, pressed or minced
2 tomatoes, chopped
1 small sweet potato, peeled and
   chunked
2 medium red-skinned potatoes,
   cut in large chunks
1 carrot, sliced ¼ inch thick
¼ cup long grain brown rice
1 bay leaf

1 tsp. ground cumin
2 tbsp. low sodium soy sauce
2 small zucchini, sliced ½ inch
   thick
¼ head cabbage, cut in large
   pieces
¼ cup chopped fresh coriander

### AVOCADO SALSA (optional)

1 ripe avocado
3 tbsp. chopped fresh coriander
⅓ cup water

¾ tsp. Tabasco
½ tsp. vinegar
1 tsp. low sodium soy sauce

SOUP: Place the water in a large soup pot. Add onions, garlic, tomatoes, potatoes, carrots, rice and seasonings. Bring to boil, cover, reduce heat to medium and cook about 30 minutes. Add cabbage, zucchini and coriander. Cook an additional 30 minutes.

Serve in large soup bowls, use fork and spoon to eat. Pass avocado salsa to spoon over the top of individual servings, if desired.

SALSA: Peel and pit the avocado and place in blender jar. Add remaining ingredients and blend until smooth. (This should be done just before serving so the avocado does not turn brown). Place in a bowl and use a small amount as a garnish for the Colombian Soup, with each person using as much or as little as they wish.

## NORTH AFRICAN BEAN SOUP

### SERVINGS: 8

PREPARATION TIME: 20 mins.    COOKING TIME: 2½ hrs.

| | |
|---|---|
| 2 cups dry white beans | 2 tbsp. low sodium soy sauce |
| 8 cups water | dash or two of cayenne pepper |
| 2 onions, chopped | 1 tsp. ground cumin |
| 2 cloves garlic, minced | ½ tsp. allspice |
| ⅓ cup chopped, fresh coriander | 1 tsp. paprika |
| 2 carrots, sliced | dash black pepper |
| 2 potatoes, chunked | 2 tomatoes, chopped |

Cook beans in the water in a large pot for 1½ hours. Add remaining ingredients, except for the tomatoes. Cook for an additional 45 minutes. Add tomatoes, cook 15 minutes longer. Garnish with more chopped fresh coriander, if desired.

## MANHATTAN BEAN SOUP

### SERVINGS: 8

PREPARATION TIME: 30 mins.    COOKING TIME: 3 hrs.

| | |
|---|---|
| 7 cups water | 2 tbsp. low sodium soy sauce |
| 1 cup Great Northern beans | ¼ tsp. ground coriander |
| ½ cup baby lima beans | ¼ tsp. dry mustard |
| 1 onion, chopped | dash white pepper |
| 1 stalk celery, chopped | 1½ cups acceptable milk (rice, oat, |
| 1 large potato, chopped | nut, soy) |
| 1 (16 oz.) can chopped tomatoes | |

Place beans and water in a soup pot. Bring to a boil, reduce heat, cover and cook about 2 hours. Add vegetables and seasonings. Cook an additional hour. Remove 1 cup of soup and process in blender until smooth. Add milk and mix well. Add this mixture back to soup pan. Stir until heated through.

# LIMA BEAN CHOWDER

### SERVINGS: 6-8

PREPARATION TIME: 30 mins.　COOKING TIME: 2¼ hrs.

2½ cups dried baby lima beans
8 cups water
2 onions, finely chopped
2 carrots, finely chopped
2 stalks celery, chopped
2 cloves garlic, pressed
1 tbsp. parsley flakes

1 tsp. caraway seeds
1 tsp. dill weed
¼ tsp. crushed red pepper
1 (10 oz.) pkg. frozen lima beans
　(thawed)
1 cup rice, soy or nut milk

Place dried lima beans and water in a large pot. Bring to boil, boil 1 minute, remove from heat, cover and let rest 1 hour. Return to heat, add onion, carrots, celery, garlic and seasonings. Bring to boil, reduce heat, cover and cook over medium-low heat for 1 hour. Add thawed lima beans and acceptable milk. Cook an additional 15 minutes.

*Contributed by Brenda and John Uno*

# SIMPLE VEGETABLE SOUP

### SERVINGS: 8

PREPARATION TIME: 20 mins.　COOKING TIME: 1 hr.

8 cups water
4 potatoes, sliced
2 onions, sliced, or 5 leeks, sliced
4 carrots, sliced
1 tsp. fine herbs (also called Italian
　Seasoning)

¼ tsp. garlic powder
3 tbsp. Bernard Jensen's Seasoning
1 tbsp. low sodium soy sauce
　(optional)
dash of pepper (optional)

### OPTIONAL VEGETABLES:

½ lb. mushrooms, sliced
1-2 zucchini, sliced

1-2 stalks celery sliced

Place all ingredients in a large pot. Bring to boil, cover and cook over medium heat for 1 hour.

HELPFUL HINTS: May be cooked in a slow cooker. Add all ingredients at once. Cook on high for 4-6 hours. May also be pressure cooked. Cook under pressure for 15 minutes, allow to "cool" naturally, about 20 minutes.

# MOROCCAN GARBANZO SOUP

SERVINGS: 8

PREPARATION TIME: 20 mins.    COOKING TIME: 2 hrs.
(presoaked beans needed)

1¼ cups garbanzo beans
8 cups water
2 onions, chopped
2 cloves garlic, pressed
2 tbsp. chopped parsley
½ tsp. turmeric

½ tsp. ground ginger
½ tsp. cinnamon
1 (16 oz.) can tomatoes, drained
  and chopped
⅓ cup lentils
⅓ cup long grain brown rice

Soak beans overnight in 2 qts. of water. Drain. Add 8 cups fresh water, the onions, garlic and spices. Bring to a boil. Reduce heat, cover and cook over medium heat for 45 minutes. Add tomatoes, lentils and rice. Cook an additional 1¼ hrs.

# MEXICAN BEAN SOUP

SERVINGS: 6

PREPARATION TIME: 15 mins.    COOKING TIME: 3 hrs.

2 cups pinto beans
8 cups water
1 large onion, chopped
2 tsp. chili powder
½ tsp. ground oregano

½ tsp. ground cumin
2 tbsp. low sodium soy sauce
  (optional)
dash or two of Tabasco (optional)

Place beans and water in a large soup pot. Bring to a boil, reduce heat, cover and cook over medium-low heat for 1 hour. Add remaining ingredients, continue to cook for about 2 hours, until beans are tender.

HELPFUL HINTS: May be made in a slow cooker. Add all ingredients at once. Cook on high for about 6-8 hours.

# CREAMY THAI SOUP

SERVINGS: 6

PREPARATION TIME: 15 mins.    COOKING TIME: 20 mins.

4 ¼ cups water
1 onion, coarsely chopped
2 cloves garlic, pressed
1 tsp. curry powder
2 tsp. ground cumin
2 tsp. ground coriander
dash cayenne

2 tbsp. low sodium soy sauce
2 cups cauliflower, coarsely
  chopped
8 oz. firm tofu, cut in cubes
1 tbsp. lemon juice
¼ cup fresh coriander, chopped

Place ½ cup water in a large saucepan. Add onion and garlic and saute for 5 minutes. Add spices and soy sauce. Mix well. Add remaining water. Add cauliflower and tofu. Bring to a boil, reduce heat, cover and cook for 10 minutes.

Using a blender or food processor, process until smooth. Return to pan. Add lemon juice and coriander. Cook for several minutes. Serve hot.

## GOURMET ONION SOUP

SERVINGS: 6-8

PREPARATION TIME: 25 mins.    COOKING TIME: 60 mins.

2 onions , sliced into rings
2 leeks, sliced (white and light
  green)
12 green onions, sliced
¼ cup minced shallots
2 cloves garlic, crushed
2 tsp. grated fresh ginger root

1/16 tsp. cayenne pepper
2 tsp. whole wheat flour
7 cups water
1 cup white wine (or use water)
¼ cup low sodium soy sauce
1 tsp. lemon juice
fresh ground pepper
fresh chives, snipped

Saute onions in ½ cup water for 5 minutes. Add leeks, green onions, and shallots with another ½ cup water. Saute a few minutes to soften. Add garlic, ginger and cayenne. Stir a few times, then add flour and stir for a couple of minutes. Slowly mix in water, wine and soy sauce. Bring to boil, reduce heat, cover and simmer for 45 minutes.

Add lemon juice and several twists of ground pepper. Mix. Ladle into bowls and garnish with snipped chives.

## WHITE ONION BISQUE

SERVINGS: 4-6

PREPARATION TIME: 15 mins.    COOKING TIME: 40 mins.

6 large white onions, sliced
6 cups water
3 tbsp. whole wheat flour
2 tbsp. low sodium soy sauce

1 cup nut milk or soy milk
⅛ tsp. white pepper
ground nutmeg for garnish

Place onions in a large saucepan with 1 cup of the water. Cook over medium heat, stirring often until onions are very soft, about ½ hour. Stir in flour. Add remaining ingredients. Bring to a boil, stirring occasionally. Spoon into bowls, garnish with nutmeg.

## SPANISH GARBANZO SOUP

### SERVINGS: 8-10

PREPARATION TIME: 20 mins.    COOKING TIME: 3 hrs.

2 cups garbanzo beans
10 cups water
⅓ cup brown rice
1 (lb.) can tomatoes
2 onions, chopped
1 green pepper, chopped
2 cloves garlic, crushed
1 tsp. chili powder

½ tsp. oregano
½ tsp. ground cumin
1/16 tsp. powdered Saffron
    (optional)
black pepper (optional)
2 tbsp. low sodium soy sauce
1 (14 oz.) can artichoke hearts
    (drained, water packed)

Cook the garbanzos in the water for 2 hours. Then add the remaining ingredients except the artichokes and cook an additional hour. Add the artichokes about 15 minutes before the soup is finished cooking.

HELPFUL HINTS: Reheats well.

## HEARTY VEGETABLE SOUP

### SERVINGS: 10-12

PREPARATION TIME: 30-40 mins.    COOKING TIME: 1½ hrs.
(cooked beans and grains needed)

4 onions, chopped
3 cloves garlic, pressed
2 green peppers, chopped
1 cup water
1 tsp. basil
1 tsp. oregano
1 tsp. ground cumin

1 tbsp. chili powder
4 cups chopped, canned tomatoes
    and their juice
1 cup tomato sauce
4 cups water
1 cup red wine (optional)
3 med. potatoes, chunked

3 med. carrots, sliced
1 cup green beans
1 cup corn kernels
1 cup cooked whole grains
1½ cups cooked beans
  (pinto, kidney,
  garbanzo, white)

2 cups shredded leafy greens
  (kale, spinach, collards, etc.)

garnishes: chopped green onions,
  chopped parsley,
  chopped chives

Using a large soup pot, saute the onions, garlic and green pepper in 1 cup water for 5 minutes. Add the spices and cook and stir a few more minutes. Add tomatoes, tomato sauce, additional water and the optional wine. Also add some fresh ground black pepper, if desired. Cover and cook over medium heat about 15 minutes to blend flavors. Add potatoes and carrots, cook for 30 minutes. Add green beans and corn, cook for 15 minutes. Add cooked grains and beans, plus greens. Cook an additional 15 minutes. Garnish with chopped parsley, chives or green onions just before serving, if desired.

HELPFUL HINTS: This makes a large amount but it freezes well. Some of the vegetables could be omitted, if desired, or other vegetables may be substituted. This recipe can also be halved to make a lesser quantity.

## NINE STAPLES SOUP

### SERVINGS: 10-12

PREPARATION TIME: 15 mins.    COOKING TIME: 3 hrs.

12 cups water
½ cup pinto beans
½ cup white beans
½ cup black beans
½ cup pink beans
½ cup lima beans
½ cup garbanzo beans
½ cup lentils

¼ cup barley
¼ cup whole wheat berries
2 bay leaves
3 onions, chopped
1 tsp. ground oregano
1 tsp. ground cumin
2 tsp. chili powder
dash or two black pepper (optional)

Place all ingredients in a large soup pot. Bring to boil. Cover. Reduce heat. Cook over medium heat for 3 hrs. Garnish with some chopped fresh coriander before serving, if desired.

HELPFUL HINTS: Add some chopped vegetables an hour before serving time; carrots, potatoes, celery, etc. May be made in a slow cooker. Reduce water to 10 cups. Cook on high for 8-10 hours.

# ITALIAN PASTA SOUP

SERVINGS: 6-8

PREPARATION TIME: 30 mins.    COOKING TIME: 1½ hrs.
(cooked beans needed)

1 cup dried split peas
9 cups water
1 onion, chopped
2 potatoes, chunked
2 carrots, sliced
1 clove garlic, crushed
1 (16 oz.) can cut tomatoes
   in juice
1 bay leaf
1 tsp. oregano

1 tsp. basil
1 tbsp. parsley flakes
¼ tsp. black pepper
   (optional)
1½ cups cooked beans
   (kidney, garbanzo, etc.)
1 cup uncooked whole grain
   macaroni
2 cups chopped fresh spinach
   (optional)

Place split peas and water in a large pot. Bring to a boil, reduce heat, cover and cook for 30 minutes. Add onion, potatoes, carrots, garlic, tomatoes and seasonings. Cook an additional 40 minutes. Add beans and macaroni. Cook 15 minutes longer. Add spinach. Heat for 5 minutes.

Remove bay leaf before serving.

*Contributed by Bessie Daniels*

# FASSOLADA
# (GREEK BEAN SOUP)

SERVINGS: 6

PREPARATION TIME: 30 mins.    COOKING TIME: 2 hrs.

2 cups white beans or
   black-eyed peas
2 qts. water
1 large onion, finely chopped
2 stalks celery,
   finely chopped
2 carrots,
   finely chopped

2 cloves garlic, crushed
1 tbsp. chopped parsley
2 bay leaves
dash of dried mint
½ tsp. fines herbs
   (Italian Seasoning Blend)
1 (8 oz.) can tomato sauce
2 tbsp. low sodium soy sauce

Soak beans overnight in water to cover. OR place beans and water in a large pot, bring to a boil, boil 1 minute, remove from heat and let rest 1 hour. Drain and set aside. Saute onion, celery, carrots, garlic, parsley, bay leaves, mint and herbs in ½ cup water for 10 minutes. Add tomato sauce, beans, soy sauce and remaining water. Bring to a boil, reduce heat, cover and cook for 2 hours or until beans are tender.

# MEXICAN GAZPACHO

SERVINGS: makes 2 qts.

PREPARATION TIME: 30 mins. CHILLING TIME: 2 hrs.

1 (46 oz.) can tomato juice
1 cucumber, peeled
1 zucchini
1 stalk celery
1 to 2 green onions

½ green pepper
3 large tomatoes
1 cup Mexican salsa
¼ to ½ tsp. Tabasco sauce

Chop all the vegetables in large chunks. Using a blender, process the ingredients in batches in a small amount of the tomato juice. Transfer the blended ingredients to a large bowl. When all ingredients are blended, mix together well. Transfer to a large covered jar or pitcher. Refrigerate at least 2 hours to blend flavors.

HELPFUL HINTS: This can easily be prepared early in the day or even a day or two ahead of when you plan to serve it. Makes an excellent snack food for hot summer days.

When using as a first course for a large dinner, pass some finely chopped vegetables to garnish each individual bowl of soup. Some suggestions are: finely chopped green onions, chopped cucumbers, chopped green peppers, chopped celery, sliced radishes.

# RUSSIAN BORSCHT

SERVINGS: 6

PREPARATION TIME: 30 mins.    COOKING TIME: 1¼ hrs.

6 cups water
1 cup peeled, thinly sliced beets
1 onion, chopped
2 carrots, thinly sliced
2 large potatoes, peeled and diced

4 cups coarsely shredded red
   cabbage
½ tsp. dill weed
fresh ground pepper
2 tbsp. lemon juice
2 tbsp. honey

Place the water in a large soup pot. Add beets, onions, carrots, potatoes and cabbage. Bring to a boil. Cover, reduce heat to medium and cook for 60 minutes. Add seasonings. Cook an additional 15 minutes.

May be served hot or cold.

*Contributed by Bill McDougall*

## CREAM OF BROCCOLI SOUP

### SERVINGS: 6

PREPARATION TIME: 30 mins.    COOKING TIME: 30 mins.

1 large onion, chopped
2 stalks celery, chopped
1 large bunch broccoli, chopped (6 cups)
4 cups water

2 tbsp. low sodium soy sauce
1 tsp. curry powder
½ tsp. garlic powder
dash white pepper

In a medium sized pan, saute the onions and celery in about ½ cup water until soft, about 5 minutes. Add broccoli, the rest of the water and the seasonings. Cook over medium heat until broccoli is tender, about 15-20 minutes.

Puree the soup in 2 batches in a blender. Place in a clean pan. Heat through. Serve hot.

Garnish with some chopped parsley, chives, or coriander if desired.

*Contributed by Chef Teruya of the Outrigger Canoe Club*

## COUNTRY VEGETABLE SOUP

### SERVINGS: 6-8

PREPARATION TIME: 35 mins.    COOKING TIME: 1 to 1½ hrs.

1 cup dried red beans
1 cup dried garbanzo beans
2 medium potatoes, thinly sliced
2 leeks, thinly sliced
2 medium onions, thinly sliced
1 carrot, thinly sliced
3 celery ribs, thinly sliced
1 small turnip, thinly sliced

3 cloves garlic, chopped
3 whole tomatoes, fresh, skinned, seeded, and chopped
2 bay leaves
2 cloves
1 pinch thyme
1 pinch marjoram
white pepper (optional)

Soak beans separately overnight in 1 quart water each. Cook separately in the soaking liquid. They will take approximately 1 to 1½ hours to cook.

Place the remaining ingredients in a large soup pot with 2½ quarts of water. Bring to a boil, cover, reduce heat and simmer for 1 hour. Add cooked beans. Heat through. Garnish with roughly chopped fresh parsley or sweet basil before serving.

*Contributed by Betty Fernie*
## BASIL BEAN SOUP

SERVINGS: 6-8

PREPARATION TIME: 30 mins.    COOKING TIME: 2½ hrs.

6 cups water
1 lb. white kidney beans
1 lb. zucchini, diced
2 medium white turnips, diced
1 large potato, diced
4 medium carrots, diced

2 celery stalks, diced
2 onions, diced
1 (1 lb.) can tomatoes
1 bay leaf
1 tbsp. basil
2 tbsp. parsley

Place beans and water in a large soup pan. Bring to a boil, cover, reduce heat to medium and cook for 1½ hours. Add remaining ingredients. Continue to cook an additional hour or until beans and vegetables are tender.

## SOUTH OF THE BORDER SOUP

SERVINGS: 8

PREPARATION TIME: 30 mins.    COOKING TIME: 60 mins.

6 cups water
1½ cups Picante sauce
2 cloves garlic, crushed
2 onions, cut into wedges
5 carrots, sliced ½ inch thick
4 medium potatoes, cut into large
  chunks
½ cup long grain brown rice

1 green pepper, cut into ½ inch
  pieces
1 rib celery, cut into ½ inch slices
½ small cabbage, shredded
2 cups corn kernels
2 tomatoes, cut into wedges
fresh chopped coriander

Place 6 cups water in a large soup pot. Add picante sauce (Either mild, medium or hot depending on your taste buds). Add garlic, onions, carrots, potatoes and rice. Cook over medium heat for 30 minutes. Add green pepper, celery, cabbage and corn. Cook 20 minutes longer. Add tomatoes and coriander (if desired), heat through. Serve in large bowls. Garnish with lemon wedges, if desired. Pass more hot picante sauce to spoon on at the table.

## MUSHROOM SOUP

SERVINGS: 6

PREPARATION TIME: 15 mins.    COOKING TIME: 30 mins.

1½ lbs. mushrooms, sliced
1 onion, thinly sliced
1 large clove garlic, crushed
2 bay leaves
¾ cup white wine (or apple juice)
5 cups water

3 to 4 tbsp. low sodium soy sauce
1 tsp. honey
1½ tsp. basil
2 tsp. dill weed
1 tsp. paprika
fresh ground black pepper

Combine all ingredients in large saucepan. Bring to a boil, reduce heat, cover and simmer for about 30 minutes.

## GOLDEN ONION SOUP

### SERVINGS: 4-6

PREPARATION TIME: 15 mins.   COOKING TIME: 40 mins.

6 large yellow onions, thinly sliced
6 cups water
1 clove garlic, pressed
2 tbsp. low sodium soy sauce
1 tsp. ground coriander

¼ tsp. turmeric
1/16 tsp. white pepper
2½ tbsp. whole wheat flour
⅓ cup sherry or apple juice

Place onions in a large saucepan with 1 cup of the water. Cook over medium heat, stirring often until onions are very soft and limp, about 30 minutes. Add garlic, soy sauce, coriander, turmeric and white pepper. Mix in well. Stir in flour. Add the remaining water and the sherry. Bring to a boil, stirring occasionally. Serve very hot.

## CARROT SOUP

### SERVINGS: 4

PREPARATION TIME: 15 mins.   COOKING TIME: 20 mins.

3 large carrots, chopped
1 small onion, chopped
1 potato, peeled and chopped
4 cups water

1 tsp. honey
¼ tsp. ground ginger
⅛ tsp. ground nutmeg
Several dashes white pepper

Combine all ingredients in a saucepan. Bring to a boil, reduce heat, cover and simmer for 15 minutes. In a blender or food processor, blend soup until smooth. Return to pan, heat through, garnish with chopped fresh parsley or coriander.

HELPFUL HINT: This makes a good appetizer soup. To make it into a more hearty dinner soup, add 1-2 cups of cooked brown rice.

# GREEN ONION SOUP

SERVINGS: 6

PREPARATION TIME: 20 mins.    COOKING TIME: 30 mins.

6 large leeks
6 ½ cups water
2½ tbsp. whole wheat flour
⅛ tsp. sage
⅛ tsp. oregano
½ tsp. parsley flakes

2 tbsp. low sodium soy sauce
⅛ tsp. white pepper
3 cups green onions, thinly sliced,
   including tops
½ cup white wine (optional)
1 tbsp. lemon juice
dash or two of Tabasco

Prepare leeks by cutting off root ends and tough green stems. Split lengthwise and rinse out well. Thinly slice and rinse again if necessary.

Place leeks in a large pot with ½ cup water. Cook and stir over medium heat until leeks are very soft, about 20 minutes. Add more water if necessary. Stir in flour. Add remaining water and spices. Bring to a boil, add green onions and wine (if desired.) Cook 5 minutes. Stir in lemon juice and Tabasco. Serve garnished with fresh lemon slices.

# WILD RICE SOUP

SERVINGS: 8-10

PREPARATION TIME: 30 mins.    COOKING TIME: 1¼ hrs.

2 onions, sliced
4 stalks celery, sliced
3 carrots, sliced
1 cup sliced green onions
2 oz. chopped pimiento
1 tbsp. dillweed
2 bay leaves
½ tsp. turmeric
½ tsp. ground cumin
¼ tsp. garlic powder

fresh ground pepper (several twists)
⅛ tsp. horseradish powder
½ tsp. poultry seasoning
12½ cups water
3 tbsp. low sodium soy sauce
¾ cup wild rice
½ cup brown rice
1 lb. fresh mushrooms, sliced

Saute onions, celery, carrots, green onions and pimiento in ½ cup water for 5 minutes. Stir in spices and mix well. Add remaining water, the soy sauce, and both kinds of rice. Bring to a boil, reduce heat, cover and simmer for 1 hour. Add sliced mushrooms, cook an additional 10 minutes. Serve hot.

## WINTER GRAINS SOUP

SERVINGS: 8-10

PREPARATION TIME: 30 mins.    COOKING TIME: 1½ hrs.

| | |
|---|---|
| 10 cups water | 1 tsp. basil |
| ½ cup whole wheat berries | ½ tsp. cumin |
| ⅔ cup lentils | 1½ cups chopped onion |
| ½ cup brown rice | ½ cup sliced carrots |
| ¼ cup barley | ½ cup sliced celery |
| ¼ cup parsley flakes | ½ cup cubed potatoes |
| 1 tbsp. onion powder | 3 tbsp. low sodium soy sauce |
| ½ tbsp. garlic powder | 1 cup frozen corn kernels |
| | 1 cup frozen peas |

Place the water in a large soup pot. Add wheat berries, lentils, brown rice, barley, parsley and spices. Bring to a boil and cook over medium heat for 60 minutes. Add the fresh chopped vegetables, cook 20 minutes. Then add the frozen vegetables and cook an additional 10 minutes.

## POTATO CHOWDER

SERVINGS: 10

PREPARATION TIME: 30 mins.    COOKING TIME: 55 mins.

| | |
|---|---|
| 1 large onion, coarsely chopped | 2 tbsp. low sodium soy sauce |
| 3 stalks celery, sliced | 1 tsp. basil |
| 1 green pepper, chopped | ½ tsp. paprika |
| 2 carrots, sliced | ¼ tsp. pepper |
| 2 cloves garlic, crushed | 1 28 oz. can chopped tomatoes in |
| 6 ½ cups water | their juice |
| 4 large potatoes, cubed | |

Place onion, celery, green pepper, carrots and garlic in a large soup pot with ½ cup water. Saute for 5 minutes, until vegetables are crisp-tender. Add potatoes, soy sauce, basil, paprika, pepper, and remaining water. Bring to a boil, reduce heat, cover and cook over medium-low heat for 30 minutes. Add tomatoes, cover and cook an additional 15 minutes.

## CELLOPHANE NOODLE SOUP

SERVINGS: 4-6

PREPARATION TIME: 30 mins.    COOKING TIME: 20 mins.

3-4 oz. cellophane noodles
("long rice" or bean threads)
1 onion, sliced
2 carrots, thinly sliced diagonally
2 garlic cloves, crushed
1 tsp. grated fresh gingerroot
4 ½ cups water
¼ cup low sodium soy sauce
⅛ cup sherry or apple juice
1 cup sliced broccoli

1 cup watercress leaves
1 cup sliced mushrooms
1 cup snow peas, left whole
1 cup Enoki mushrooms,
cleaned & trimmed (or use
canned straw mushrooms)
1 tsp. rice vinegar
pinch red pepper flakes
2 green onions, chopped

Place cellophane noodles in a bowl. Cover with cool water. Let stand for 5 minutes. Drain. Place onions and carrots in a large soup pot with ½ cup water. Cook and stir for a few minutes. Add garlic and ginger and cook a few minutes longer. Add remaining water, sherry and soy sauce. Bring to a boil. Add broccoli, watercress, mushrooms, and snow peas. Bring to boil again. Add cellophane noodles. Cook about 5 minutes over low heat. Vegetables should be crisp-tender. Stir in vinegar and red pepper flakes. Serve at once. Pass the chopped green onions at the table for garnish.

HELPFUL HINTS: Cellophane noodles can be found in Oriental food stores. Some supermarkets may also carry them, especially when they have an Oriental section. These noodles are also called bean threads or "long rice." They are made from bean starch and water.

## MISO SOUP

### SERVINGS: 4

PREPARATION TIME: 20 mins.    COOKING TIME: 20 mins.

4 cups Kombu stock
(recipe elsewhere in book)
½ cup white miso
¼ lb. firm tofu,
cut into ½ inch cubes

1 tbsp. low sodium soy sauce
1 bunch green onions,
finely chopped

Take about ¼ cup of stock and add it to the miso in a small bowl. Mix well until there are no lumps. Add miso mixture and tofu to stock. Bring to a boil. Remove from heat immediately. Stir in soy sauce. Serve at once. Pass green onions at the table to garnish the soup.

## WON TON SOUP

### SERVINGS: 10-12

PREPARATION TIME: 1½ hrs.    COOKING TIME: 20 mins.

WON TON:

60-70 won ton wrappers
1 cup Chinese cabbage,
  finely chopped
2 green onions, minced
¼ cup celery, finely chopped
¼ cup bamboo shoots,
  finely chopped

¼ cup water chestnuts,
  finely chopped
½ lb. tofu, crumbled
1 tbsp. grated gingerroot
1 tbsp low sodium soy sauce
1 tbsp. sherry (optional)
¼ tsp. garlic
dash of white pepper

Place all ingredients (except the wrappers) in a wok or a sauce pan. Add about 1 tablespoon of water. Saute over medium heat for 5 minutes, stirring constantly. Cool. Stuff the won ton wraps with about 1 teaspoon of filling in each. Wrap as follows: Fill a small bowl with water. Place next to your work surface. Take one wrapper at a time and place on a flat surface with the pointed end toward you. Place filling in center. Moisten top 2 edges with water on your finger tips from the bowl. Fold wrap in half to make a triangle. Then fold the top point down to make what looks like a long roll. Then take the 2 ends and press gently to close, sealing with a dab of water. Place on a large piece of waxed paper. Repeat until all are filled.

SOUP BROTH:

18-20 cups of vegetable stock,
  Kombu stock (recipe in this
  volume) or water to which some
  pure vegetable seasoning and a
  little soy sauce have been added

1 bunch green onions, sliced
1 bunch watercress, use sprigs and
  leaves only

Bring broth to a boil. Add green onions and watercress. Cook for 15 minutes. Gently slip the won tons into the broth using a large spoon. Cook for an additional 5 minutes. Serve at once.

HELPFUL HINTS: Won ton wrappers are made from flour and water. I have seen some made from whole wheat flour in some natural food stores. Otherwise, you may need to go to an oriental market to buy them. This makes a large amount, but it is quite time consuming to prepare, so save this recipe for special occasions. Be careful not to get your wrappers too wet when sealing them or they will stick to the waxed paper. Check the ones you have finished to make sure they are not sticking by occasionally moving them gently. The Won Tons may be prepared ahead of time, then slipped into the soup broth just before serving.

# POTATO AND BEAN SOUP

### SERVINGS: 6-8

PREPARATION TIME: 20 mins.    COOKING TIME: 45 mins.
(cooked beans needed)

8 cups potato, chopped
1 onion, chopped
6 cups water
4 cups cooked pinto beans

1 tbsp. low sodium soy sauce
1 tsp. paprika
1 tsp. savory
fresh ground pepper

Place the potatoes and onions in the water in a large soup pot.
Cook until soft, about 30 minutes. Add 3 cups of the beans, the soy sauce, paprika and savory. Heat through. Blend soup in batches until smooth. Return to pan. Stir in remaining beans and season with fresh ground pepper to taste. Heat through and serve.

*Contributed by Susan Krueger*

# CREAMED TOFU SOUP

### SERVINGS: 4-6

PREPARATION TIME: 30 mins.    COOKING TIME: 15 mins.

16 oz. firm tofu
2 cups cooked vegetables (asparagus, spinach, or a mixture of zucchini, celery and onions
2 cups water (use vegetable cooking water)
½ tsp. dill weed
½ tsp. garlic powder
½ tsp. pepper

Place the cooked vegetables in a blender with 1 cup of the water.
Blend until smooth. Add half of the tofu, crumbled up to make blending easier. (Add more of the water if necessary). Blend until very smooth. Pour into a sauce pan. Add seasonings and remaining water. Mix well. Cube the remaining tofu and add to the creamy mixture. Heat over low until heated thoroughly.

HELPFUL HINTS: This is also good made with cabbage as the vegetable and some curry powder added to the seasonings.

# ZUCCHINI VELVET SOUP

### SERVINGS: 6

PREPARATION TIME: 15 mins.    COOKING TIME: 30 mins.

1 onion
4 cups water
4 large zucchini, cut in chunks
½ cup oatmeal

⅓ cup fresh dill, finely chopped
2 tbsp. low sodium soy sauce
dash or two of white pepper

Cook the onion in ½ cup of the water in a medium saucepan for 5 minutes. Add the remaining water, and the rest of the ingredients.

Bring to a boil, cover, simmer about 20 minutes. Process in blender, small amounts at a time, until velvety smooth. Serve warm. Garnish with more fresh dill, if desired.

*Contributed by Lee Knight*

## SHERRIED TOMATO SOUP

### SERVINGS: 4

PREPARATION TIME: 15 mins.    COOKING TIME: 20 mins.

⅓ cup chopped onion
⅓ cup shredded carrot
4 tsp. arrowroot (or cornstarch)
dash ground nutmeg
3 cups tomato juice
1 cup water

¼ cup dry sherry
2 tbsp. snipped parsley
2 tsp. frozen apple juice
concentrate
1 tsp. low sodium soy sauce
(optional)

Cook onion and shredded carrot in a small amount of water until tender about 5 minutes. Add arrowroot or cornstarch and nutmeg. Mix. Add tomato juice and water. Cook and stir until mixture is thickened and bubbly. Stir in sherry, parsley, apple juice and soy sauce (if desired). Simmer uncovered for 5 minutes.

HELPFUL HINTS: If you have some leftover grains, a ½ cup of cooked barley or brown rice makes a nice addition to this soup.

# Salads

## CARROT ORANGE SALAD

SERVINGS: 6

PREPARATION TIME: 15 mins.     CHILLING TIME: 2 hrs.

¾ cup raisins
1 lb carrots, grated
1 orange, peeled and chopped
2 tbsp. lemon juice

2 tbsp. orange juice
1-2 tsp. honey
½ tsp. cinnamon

Soak raisins in hot water for ½ hour. Drain. Combine all ingredients. Mix well. Cover. Chill for about 2 hours to blend flavors.

*Contributed by Ruth Heidrich*
## COLD BROWN RICE SALAD

SERVINGS: 12-15

PREPARATION TIME: 15 mins.     CHILLING TIME: 2 hrs.
(cooked rice needed)

2 tart green apples, cored and
  cubed
4 green onions, chopped
½ lb. mushrooms, sliced

1 large red or green pepper, sliced
4 cups cooked brown rice
¼ to ½ cup white wine vinegar

Mix all ingredients in a large bowl. Cover and refrigerate until well chilled.

## VEGETABLE SALAD

SERVINGS: 6-8

PREPARATION TIME: 45 mins.     CHILLING TIME: 2 hrs.

SALAD:

2 cups cauliflower florets
2 cups Brussels sprouts, cleaned
and left whole
2 cups thinly sliced carrots
1½ cup thinly sliced radishes

1 cup snow peas, trimmed and cut
in half
½ cup pitted black olices (optional)
½ cup sliced green onions
⅓ cup finely chopped parsley

DRESSING:

¼ cup water
¼ cup white wine vinegar
2 tbsp. Dijon mustard

½ tsp. oregano
1 clove garlic, pressed
freshly ground pepper

Steam cauliflower, Brussels sprouts, and carrots until crisp-tender. Combine steamed ingredients with the radishes, snow peas, olives, green onions and parsley in a large bowl.

Combine the dressing ingredients together and mix well. Pour over the vegetables and toss to coat well. Cover and refrigerate at least 2 hours before serving. Stir occasionally to blend flavors.

HELPFUL HINTS: May be prepared ahead, but do not add radishes until 2 hours before serving.

*Contributed by Linda DuPuy*

## LINDA'S NOODLE SALAD

SERVINGS: 4

PREPARATION TIME: 30 mins.    CHILLING TIME: 2 hrs.

2 cups uncooked spinach noodles
¼ cup sliced black olives
¼ cup sliced green olives
⅛ cup chopped pimiento

¾ cup Artichoke hearts, quartered
(canned without oil)
⅓ to ½ cup oil free dressing

Cook noodles in boiling water until tender, 8-10 minutes.
Combine with other ingredients. Toss gently to mix. Chill to blend flavors.

HELPFUL HINTS: This may also be made without olives to lower the fat content. The oil free dressing can also be omitted. Use some fresh pressed garlic (a clove or two), a small amount of vinegar, and some fresh ground black pepper instead.

## GARBANZO SALAD

SERVINGS: 8

PREPARATION TIME: 30 mins.    COOKING TIME: 2-3 hrs.

2½ cups garbanzo beans
3 medium potatoes, peeled and
  chopped
3 carrots, sliced ¼ inch thick
4 onions, sliced ¼ inch thick
4 cloves garlic, pressed

⅓ cup red wine vinegar
1 tbsp. dried dillweed
1 tbsp. low sodium soy sauce
1 tbsp. natural Worcestershire
  sauce
fresh ground pepper

Soak beans overnight in water to cover, or bring to a boil, boil 1 minute, remove from heat, cover and let rest one hour. Drain. Cover with fresh water. Cook in boiling water until fairly tender, at least 1½ hours. Add potatoes and carrots, cook about 30 minutes longer. Place onion slices on top of bean mixture, cover and steam until wilted, about 5 minutes. Drain. Place in large bowl. Stir in garlic, vinegar, dillweed, soy sauce and Worcestershire sauce. Add fresh ground pepper to taste. Mix well.

Serve warm or cold.

## BAKED POTATO SALAD

SERVINGS: 4

PREPARATION TIME: 30 mins.    COOKING TIME: 1¼ hrs.

4 potatoes
4 cups coarsely shredded lettuce
2 cups sliced green beans, cooked
2 tomatoes, chopped

½ cup celery, thinly sliced
½ cup radishes, thinly sliced
¼ cup green onions, chopped

Wash potatoes, prick with a fork and bake at 400 degrees until done. Cook green beans in a small amount of water until just tender. Drain. Set aside. (Use frozen green beans, if desired, and thaw in cold water. It is not necessary to cook these, unless you wish to).

Combine lettuce, tomatoes, celery, radishes, onions and cooked beans. Chill. To serve, slice baked potatos in half, then cover with some salad mixture. Top all of this with your choice of no-oil salad dressing. Some good ones are: Lemon-garlic dressing, French tomato dressing, Vinegar dressing or one of your favorites, homemade or store-bought.

## COLORFUL COLESLAW

SERVINGS: 6

PREPARATION TIME: 20-30 mins.    CHILLING TIME: 2 hrs.

2 cups shredded green cabbage
2 cups shredded red cabbage
½ cup diced carrot

¼ cup chopped parsley
3 tbsp. cider vinegar
1 tbsp. Dijon mustard

½ cup diced celery
½ cup diced green pepper
½ cup chopped apple
½ cup diced, peeled cucumber
¼ cup finely chopped green onions

½ tbsp. low sodium soy sauce
1 tsp. honey
¼ tsp. caraway seeds
¼ tsp. celery seed

Mix vegetables together in a large bowl. Mix vinegar, mustard, soy sauce and honey together. Pour over vegetables. Spinkle seeds on top. Toss to mix well. Chill for about 2 hours to blend flavors.

HELPFUL HINTS: If you have a food processor this can be prepared quite quickly.

## LENTIL SALAD

### SERVINGS: 4-6

PREPARATION TIME: 30 mins.  COOKING TIME: 30 mins.
CHILLING TIME: 3 hrs.

SALAD:

1 cup lentils
4 cups water
1 cup grated carrots

⅔ cup onions, finely chopped
½ cup fresh parsley, finely chopped
1 clove garlic, crushed

DRESSING:

1 tbsp. water
2 tbsp. red wine vinegar
2 tsp. Dijon mustard
½ tsp. oregano

1 tsp. natural Worcestershire sauce
  (no anchovies)
1 tbsp. low sodium soy sauce
¼ tsp. black pepper

Cook the lentils in the water for 30 minutes, until tender but still firm. Drain. Combine with the rest of the salad ingredients. Mix the dressing ingredients together. Pour over the salad. Toss to mix. Refrigerate at least 3 hours to blend flavors.

## RICE AND CORN SALAD

### SERVINGS: 6-8

PREPARATION TIME: 20 mins.  COOKING TIME: none
(cooked rice needed)

SALAD:

2 cups cooked brown rice
2 cups frozen corn kernels
1 tomato, coarsely chopped
½ cup chopped green pepper

½ cup chopped green onions
½ cup sliced black olives (optional)
¼ cup finely chopped fresh
  coriander, parsley or dill

DRESSING:

2 tbsp. wine vinegar
2 tbsp. water
2 tbsp. low sodium soy sauce

½ tsp. Dijon mustard
several dashes Tabasco sauce
  (optional)

SALAD: Thaw corn under cold running water. Mix with brown rice, tomato, green pepper, green onions, olives and coriander, parsley or dill.

DRESSING: In a small jar or bowl, mix vinegar, water, soy sauce, mustard and Tabasco sauce. Pour over salad. Mix well.

Cover and chill for at least 2 hours before serving for best flavor. If you're in a rush, it may also be served soon after mixing.

### *Contributed by Carol Emerick*
## LIMA BEAN SALAD

#### SERVINGS: 3

#### PREPARATION TIME: 5 mins.   COOKING TIME: 1½ hrs.

½ lb. lima beans
1 clove garlic, minced

juice of 1 lemon

Place beans in saucepan with water to cover. Cook until tender, about 1½ hours. Drain. Add garlic and lemon juice and mix well. Serve hot or cold.

### *Contributed by Carol Emerick*
## SYRIAN POTATO SALAD

#### SERVINGS: 4

#### PREPARATION TIME: 15 mins.   COOKING TIME: 45 mins.

1 lb. potatoes
juice of 1 lemon
1 onion, chopped
1 tsp. cold water

1 tbsp. chopped parsley
2 tomatoes, sliced
1 tbsp. dried mint
several sliced black olives

Boil potatoes until just tender. Peel and cube. Add lemon juice, onion and water. Mix well. Garnish with parsley, tomatoes, olives and mint.

# SUPER SPROUT SALAD

### SERVINGS: 4-6

PREPARATION TIME: 20 mins.    COOKING TIME: none

SALAD:

2 cups mixed sprouts (lentils, pea, aduki, etc.)
3-4 green onions, sliced
1 stalk celery, sliced

2.2 oz. jar chopped pimientos
3/4 cup sliced mushrooms
3-4 tablespoons chopped fresh coriander or parsley

DRESSING:

2 tsp. Dijon mustard
1 tbsp. water
2 tbsp. white wine vinegar

1 tsp. Worcestershire sauce
1 tbsp. low sodium soy sauce
1/4 tsp. black pepper

Mix salad ingredients in a large bowl.

Place the mustard and the water in a small bowl and mix well. Add remaining ingredients and mix, then pour over the sprout salad. Toss to coat. Refrigerate before serving.

# QUICK PASTA TOSS

### SERVINGS: 6

PREPARATION TIME: 10 mins.    COOKING TIME: 10 mins.

2 cups uncooked elbow macaroni or other pasta
(whole wheat or spinach)

4 cups chopped vegetables
1/2 to 2/3 cups oil-free dressing

Cook macaroni in boiling water until just tender, 8-10 minutes.
Steam vegetables until tender, 10-15 minutes. Mix together. Add dressing, toss to coat. Serve hot or cold.

HELPFUL HINTS: Chop the vegetables quite small so they cook quickly. Frozen vegetables may also be used. This dish is very adaptable to changes and can be different each time you serve it. Use either all one kind of vegetable or a combination of your favorites.

# VEGETABLES A LA GRECQUE

SERVINGS: 8

PREPARATION TIME: 60 mins.     CHILLING TIME: 4 hrs.

**COOKING SAUCE:**

3 ½ cups water
⅓ cup lemon juice
¾ cup white wine
2 bay leaves
2 cloves garlic, cut in half

1 shallot or 2 green onions,
   chopped
6 black peppercorns
1 tsp. thyme leaves
1 tsp. tarragon
¼ cup chopped fresh parsley

**VEGETABLES:**

3 carrots, sliced lengthwise, ½ inch
   wide, about 3 inches long
2 zucchini, sliced lengthwise, ½
   inch wide, about 3 inches long
3 leeks, trimmed—leave 1 inch
   green top, then cut in half
   lengthwise

½ lb. green beans, sliced 3 inches
   long
½ lb. mushrooms, cut in half
10 boiling onions, cleaned

Combine water, lemon juice, wine and bay leaves in large pan.
Place garlic, shallot, peppercorns, herbs and parsley in a cheesecloth and tie
closed. Add to pan. Bring to boil, reduce heat, cover and simmer for 10
minutes. Add vegetables as follows: Remove each vegetable group after
cooking for recommended time.

COOKING TIME:  Carrots:        cook 10 minutes
               Leeks:          cook 5 minutes
               Zucchini:       cook 5 minutes
               Green Beans:    cook 10 minutes
               Onions:         cook 10 minutes
               Mushrooms:      cook 5 minutes

After vegetables are cooked, remove cheesecloth bag, increase heat and cook
broth uncovered until reduced to 1 cup. Spoon over vegetables.

Arrange on platter. Garnish with chopped parsley. Serve warm or cold.

# PASTA SALAD BOWL

SERVINGS: 8

PREPARATION TIME: 30 mins.     COOKING TIME: 10 mins.
                               CHILLING TIME: 2 hrs.

4 cups whole wheat or vegetable
  pasta
1 cup broccoli or cauliflower
  flowerets
1 cup slivered carrots
20 whole fresh snow pea pods,
  trimmed

½ lb. sliced fresh mushrooms
½ pt. cherry tomatoes, cut in half
2 green onions, chopped
1 can (2¼ oz.) sliced black olives
  (optional)
1 jar (2 oz.) chopped pimiento
½ cup oil-free Italian dressing

Cook pasta in boiling water until tender, about 10 minutes. Drain. Rinse under cool water, set aside.

Steam broccoli or cauliflower, carrots and snow peas for 5 minutes.

Combine all ingredients in a large bowl. Toss to mix well. Sprinkle with some fresh ground black pepper if desired. Refrigerate at least 2 hrs. before serving.

HELPFUL HINTS: Corkscrew or spiral pasta are very attractive when used in this recipe. Vegetables used can be varied to suit your family's taste.

## THREE BEAN SALAD

SERVINGS: 8-10

PREPARATION TIME: 30 mins.    CHILLING TIME: 1-2 hrs.
(cooked beans needed)

VEGETABLES:

2 cups cooked garbanzo beans
2 cups cooked kidney beans
2 cups cooked green beans
1 red onion, sliced and separated
  into rings
2-3 stalks celery, sliced

2 carrots, grated
1 small green pepper, cut in thin
  strips
4 green onions, chopped
¼ cup chopped fresh parsley
  (optional)

SAUCE:

½ cup wine vinegar
1-2 tbsp. honey
½ tsp. dry mustard
¼ tsp. garlic powder

¼ tsp. onion powder
¼ tsp. pepper (optional)
¼ tsp. ground cumin (optional)

Combine vegetables in a large bowl. Combine sauce ingredients. Pour sauce over vegetables and mix well. Cover and chill 1-2 hours, or more, to blend flavors. (½ cup of your favorite oil-free dressing may be used in place of the sauce.)

# MARINATED CUCUMBERS

SERVINGS: 6-8

PREPARATION TIME: 15 mins.    CHILLING TIME: 2 hrs.

5 cucumbers, thinly sliced
1 onion, thinly sliced
1 cup red wine vinegar

1 to 2 tbsp. honey
2 tsp. dill weed
black pepper (optional)

Place vinegar and honey in a saucepan and heat until warm. Place cucumbers, onion, dill weed and optional pepper into a large container. Pour heated vinegar mixture over the cucumbers and onions. Mix well. Cover and refrigerate at least 2 hours. Tastes even better if eaten the following day.

# MARINATED ONIONS

SERVINGS: variable

PREPARATION TIME: 5 mins.    COOKING TIME: 5 mins.
CHILLING TIME: 1 hr.

2 onions, thinly sliced
2 tbsp. lemon juice

½ tsp. Tabasco sauce

Saute the onions in a small amount of water until limp. Transfer to a bowl. Add remaining ingredients. Cover. Chill at least 1 hour.

Use as a topping for bean dishes. Also excellent used on sandwiches.

HELPFUL HINTS: Keeps for a few days in the refrigerator. I usually keep some on hand to use in sandwiches, as they are easier on the stomach than raw onions. The amount you make can easily be adjusted. Add 1 tbsp. lemon juice and ¼ tsp. Tabasco for each additional onion.

# Main Dishes

# Vegetable Stews and Sauces

## BUDDHA'S DELIGHT

SERVINGS: 8

PREPARATION TIME: 30 mins.    COOKING TIME: 25-30 mins.

VEGETABLES:

4 cups broccoli flowerets
(or use some cauliflower with the
   broccoli)
2 cups bok choy, sliced thinly
2 cups sliced mushrooms
2 cups snow peas
1½ cups carrots, sliced

½ cup green onions, sliced
½ cup sliced water chestnuts
½ cup bamboo shoots, sliced
½ cup whole straw mushrooms
   (canned)
1 cup whole baby corn (canned)

SAUCE:

1½ cups water
2 tbsp. sherry (or apple juice)
4 tbsp. low sodium soy sauce

3 tbsp. cornstarch or arrowroot
¼ tsp. white pepper

Prepare vegetables as directed and set aside separately. Combine sauce ingredients in a separate bowl and set aside.

In a wok or a large saucepan, place about ½ cup water and a dash or two of soy sauce. Heat until it boils, then add broccoli, carrots and green onions. Cook and stir for about 10 minutes. Add mushrooms, bok choy and snow peas. Cook and stir for 5 minutes. Add bamboo shoots and water chestnuts. Cook and stir a few more minutes. Add sauce mixture to pan. Bring to a boil, stirring constantly. After mixture boils and thickens, stir in straw mushrooms and baby corn. Cook until heated thoroughly. Serve over brown rice.

HELPFUL HINTS: Buddha's delight is a popular vegetarian dish in China. There are many variations but one thing they share in common is at least 10 different vegetables are used in the preparation.

*Contributed by Dr. and Mrs. W. Shrader*

## MUSHROOM STROGONOFF

SERVINGS: 6-8

PREPARATION TIME: 30 mins.    COOKING TIME: 1¼ hrs.

1 lb. fresh mushrooms, sliced
2 pkg. (0.7 oz.) dried Shiitaki
   mushrooms
3 onions, sliced
1½ cups water
2 tbsp. low sodium soy sauce

½ cup sherry (or apple juice)
½ cup acceptable "milk"
(rice, oat, cashew, almond, or soy)
2 dashes nutmeg
4 tbsp. cornstarch or arrowroot
black pepper (optional)

Soak the Shiitaki mushrooms in hot water for 15 minutes. Squeeze out the water and slice into ¼ inch strips. Saute onions and fresh mushrooms in ½ cup water for 5 minutes. Add Shiitaki mushrooms, remaining water, soy sauce, ¼ cup sherry (or apple juice), nutmeg, and pepper, if desired. Simmer for 30 minutes over medium-low heat. Add the milk and continue to cook an additional 30 minutes, stirring occasionally. Mix the cornstarch or arrowroot in ½ cup cold water. Slowly add to the strogonoff mixture while stirring. Continue to cook and stir until thickened. Mix in the remaining ¼ cup sherry (or apple juice).

Serve over brown rice or noodles.

## ISRAELI WHEAT BERRY STEW

### SERVINGS: 8-10

PREPARATION TIME: 15 mins.    COOKING TIME: 4 hrs.

7 cups water
1½ cups Great Northern Beans
1 cup wheat berries
6 smallish potatoes, cut in half
1 large onion, sliced

4 cloves garlic, minced or pressed
5 tsp. ground cumin
4 tsp. turmeric
½ tsp. pepper (optional)

Combine all ingredients in a large pot. Cover and simmer over medium heat at least 4 hours.

HELPFUL HINTS: Wheat berries take a long time to get tender enough to chew. They add a marvelous, chewy texture to this spicy stew. This is great to make in the slow cooker because of its lengthy cooking time. It will take about 8-10 hours on the high heat setting.

## QUICK CREAMY VEGETABLES

### SERVINGS: 4

PREPARATION TIME: 10 mins.    COOKING TIME: 20 mins.

4 cups frozen vegetables
2 cups nut milk or rice milk
2 tbsp. low sodium tamari

2 tbsp. cornstarch or arrowroot
Seasonings of your choice (see
  helpful hints)

Cook the vegetables in acceptable milk until tender, about 15 minutes. Add tamari and optional seasonings of your choice. Mix cornstarch or arrowroot in ¼ cup water. Add to vegetable mixture while stirring. Cook and stir until thickened. Serve over whole wheat toast for a quick meal.

HELPFUL HINTS: This may also be made with your choice of fresh vegetables. Cut them up in small pieces so they cook quickly.

Choices for seasonings follow:

1. ½ tsp. basil
   ½ tsp. dillweed
   ½ tsp. cumin

2. ½ tsp. thyme
   ½ tsp. rosemary
   ½ tsp. marjoram

3. ½ tsp. onion powder
   ½ tsp. ground ginger
   ¼ tsp. garlic powder

4. ½ tsp. tarragon
   ½ tsp. basil
   ½ tsp. marjoram

## GRAINY VEGETABLE STEW

### SERVINGS: 8-10

PREPARATION TIME: 30 min.     COOKING TIME: 1½ hrs.

8 cups water
1 cup brown rice
¾ cup bulgur
1 onion, chopped
1 green pepper, chopped
4 potatoes, chunked
2 carrots, sliced
2 stalks broccoli, cut into bite size
  pieces

2 cloves garlic, crushed
½ bunch parsley, chopped
1 (1 lb.) can chopped tomatoes
2 tbsp. low sodium soy sauce
2 tbsp. natural Worcestershire
  sauce
2 tsp. chili powder
2 tsp. turmeric

Place all ingredients in a large pot. Bring to a boil, reduce heat, cover and cook over medium-low heat for 1½ hours.

HELPFUL HINTS: Freezes well. May be made in a slow cooker. Cook on high for 6 hours or on low for 10-12 hours.

## CHUNKY A' LA KING SAUCE

### SERVINGS: 8

PREPARATION TIME: 20 mins.     COOKING TIME: 30 mins.

2 onions, chopped
2 green peppers, chopped
½ lb mushrooms, sliced
2 celery stalks, sliced
1 (8 oz.) can sliced water chestnuts
1 (0.7 oz.) bag Shiitaki mushrooms
½ cup frozen peas
1 cup whole wheat flour
6 cups nut, soy or rice milk

1 (4 oz.) jar diced pimientos
1 (14 oz.) can artichoke hearts
  (drained and quartered)
1 (2.2 oz) can sliced ripe olives
  (drained) (optional)
⅛ tsp. white pepper
3 tbsp. low sodium soy sauce
2 tbsp. Worcestershire sauce
3 tbsp. cornstarch or arrowroot

Soak dried shiitake mushrooms in hot water to cover for 15 minutes. Drain, squeeze to press out water. Trim off stems and thinly slice.

In a large pan, cook onions, green peppers, mushrooms, celery, water chestnuts, shiitake mushrooms and peas in 1½ cups water for 10 minutes. Stir in the flour and continue to cook for a few minutes, stirring constantly. Slowly add the acceptable milk, while stirring. Cook, stirring frequently until mixture boils.

Stir in pimientos, artichoke hearts and olives. Add pepper, soy sauce and Worcestershire sauce. Mix the cornstarch or arrowroot in a small amount of cold water. Gradually add to pan while stirring. Cook and stir until mixture boils and thickens.

Serve over whole grain toast, buns, rice, baked potatoes or pasta.

HELPFUL HINTS: This makes a large amount, it keeps for several days in the refrigerator; however, it does not freeze well. To make a smaller amount, divide ingredients in half and it will make 4-5 servings.

## HEARTY POTATO VEGETABLE CURRY

### SERVINGS: 6

PREPARATION TIME: 30 mins.    COOKING TIME: 1¼ hrs.

2½ cups water
1 (16 oz.) can tomatoes, (chopped, with liquid)
3 white potatoes, chopped
1 onion, cut in wedges
2 cloves garlic, crushed
½ lb. mushrooms, cut in half
1 red or green pepper, chopped
1 green apple, peeled and diced

1 tbsp. curry powder
1 tsp. ground coriander
½ tsp. ground cumin
2 tbsp. whole wheat flour
¼ cup water
3 tbsp. chutney
1 zucchini, coarsely chopped
1½ cups frozen peas

Place water, tomatoes and the tomato liquid in a large pot. Add potatoes, onion, garlic, mushrooms, pepper, apple and spices. Bring to a boil, reduce heat to simmer.

Mix flour and water. Add to vegetable mixture. Mix in well. Cover and simmer for 30 min.

Stir in chutney, peas and zucchini. Cook uncovered 30 minutes longer.

Serve over brown rice.

56

## SPICY VEGETABLE SAUCE

SERVINGS: 4

PREPARATION TIME: 20 mins.    COOKING TIME: 25 mins.

1 onion, sliced
½ lb mushrooms, sliced
1 green pepper,chopped
2 cups another vegetable of your choice, chopped
3 cups water
3 tbsp. low sodium soy sauce

2 tbsp. natural Worcestershire sauce
1 tsp. chili powder
½ tsp. turmeric
dash or two of Tabasco sauce
4 tbsp. cornstarch or arrowroot
¼ cup chopped fresh coriander

Saute vegetables in a small amount of water for 10 minutes. Add remaining ingredients, except cornstarch or arrowroot and coriander. Cook over medium heat an additional 10 minutes. Mix cornstarch or arrowroot in ¼ cup cold water. Add to sauce while stirring. Stir until thickened and clear. Stir in fresh coriander. Serve at once over whole grain toast.

## SUMMER VEGETABLE DELIGHT

SERVINGS: 3-4

PREPARATION TIME: 20 mins.    COOKING TIME: 20 mins.

1 onion, sliced
8 medium mushrooms, sliced
1 green pepper, cut in ½ inch pieces
1 to 2 zucchini, sliced
1 cup green bean pieces

2 chopped tomatoes
1 cup corn kernels
2 tbsp. low sodium soy sauce
Seasonings (see below)

Saute onions and mushrooms in ½ cup water for 5 minutes. Add remaining vegetables and seasonings, plus ½ cup water. Cover and simmer over medium low heat for 15 minutes. Stir occasionally. Mix 1 tbsp. cornstarch or arrowroot in ¼ cup cold water. Add to vegetable mixture while stirring. Cook and stir until thickened. Serve over rice, or potatoes, or whole wheat bread.

Suggested Seasonings:
(1) ½ tsp. basil
    ½ tsp. oregano
    1 tbsp. parsley

(2) 1 tbsp. chopped fresh coriander
    ½ tsp. turmeric
    1 tsp. cumin

(3) ½ tsp. basil
  ½ tsp. dill weed
  ½ tsp. cumin
  ½ tsp. paprika

HELPFUL HINTS: This may also be made using many other vegetables.
Substitute your favorites in equivalent amounts. A fast, easy meal.

*Contributed by Phyllis Ramin*
## SYRIAN BAMYA

SERVINGS: 4-6

PREPARTAION TIME: 15 mins.    COOKING TIME: 30 mins.

1 pkg. frozen okra (thawed)     2 cans (8 oz each) tomato sauce
1 large onion, sliced           2 tsp. chopped coriander or ½ tsp
3 cloves garlic, minced           of ground coriander
1 large (20 oz) can whole tomatoes  ¼ cup lemon juice

Saute onions and garlic in a small amount of water in a non-stick pan,
stirring constantly until they brown slightly. Transfer to a saucepan, add
tomatoes, tomato sauce, okra and coriander. Mix well. Cover and cook about
15 minutes. Add lemon juice. Continue to cook an additional 10 minutes.
Serve over long grain brown rice.

## NEW ORLEANS CREOLE SAUCE

SERVINGS: 6

PREPARATION TIME: 20 mins.    COOKING TIME: 30 mins.
(cooked beans needed)

1 large onion, chopped          ¼ cup chopped fresh parsley
1 large green pepper, chopped   1 tsp. basil
3 cups okra, sliced into 1 inch  ½ tsp. Cajun Spices (recipe in this
  pieces                          Volume)
2 (16 oz.) cans chopped tomatoes  1½ tsp. Tabasco sauce
  drained                       2 cups cooked beans
2 (8 oz.) cans tomato sauce

Saute onion and green pepper in a small amount of water for 5 minutes. Add
okra, tomatoes, tomato sauce and seasonings. Cover and cook over low heat
for about 15 minutes. Add beans. Cook an additional 10 minutes.

Serve over rice, noodles, potatoes or whole grains.

HELPFUL HINTS: For a change of pace, try mixing 4 cups cooked noodles into the sauce before serving.

## VEGETABLE SPAGHETTI SAUCE

SERVINGS: 8-10

PREPARATION TIME: 30 mins.    COOKING TIME: 1½ hrs.

2 onions, chopped
½ lb. mushrooms, sliced
1 green pepper, chopped
2 carrots, sliced
2 cloves garlic, crushed
1 to 2 zucchini, chopped
1 (1 lb.) can tomatoes
1 (28 oz.) can tomato puree
1 (1 lb.) can tomato sauce

1 cup red wine (optional)
2 tsp. oregano
2 tsp. basil
¼ tsp. pepper
2 tbsp. parsley flakes
2 tbsp. honey
1 can artichoke hearts, quartered,
   drained and water packed
   (optional)

Saute the first 5 ingredients in ½ cup water for 15 minutes. Then add the chopped zucchini and the remaining ingredients except for the optional artichoke hearts. Stir to mix, then cover and cook over medium-low heat for 1 hour. Stir in the artichokes, heat for 15 more minutes. Serve over whole wheat or vegetable spaghetti noodles.

## CHINESE SPICY VEGETABLES

SERVINGS: 4

PREPARATION TIME: 30 mins.    COOKING TIME: 20 mins.
VEGETABLES:

1 onion, cut in half and sliced
1 cup celery, sliced
1½ cups chopped broccoli

½ lb. mushrooms, thinly sliced
2 cups chopped Chinese cabbage
1 cup bean sprouts

SAUCE:

4 tbsp. low sodium soy sauce
2 tbsp. cider vinegar
2 cloves, garlic—crushed
3 tbsp. chopped fresh coriander

1½ tbsp. cornstarch or arrowroot
¼ tsp. grated fresh gingerroot
¼ tsp. crushed red pepper

Mix sauce ingredients together. Set aside. Saute onions and celery in a small amount of water for 5 minutes. Add broccoli and Chinese cabbage, cook and stir for 5 more minutes. Add mushrooms. Cook and stir until soft, (5 minutes). Add bean sprouts. Stir in sauce. Heat through. Use to fill chapatis or as a topping for rice.

HELPFUL HINTS: This dish adapts well to substitutions. Try Chinese peas in place of the broccoli, Chinese white stem cabbage in the place of the celery, or try other vegetables of your choice. Reduce the amount of the crushed red pepper for a less spicy version.

## UMEBOSHI PLUM STEW

SERVINGS: 6-8

PREPARATION TIME: 30 mins.    COOKING TIME: 60 mins.

| | |
|---|---|
| 2 onions, sliced | 2 cups water |
| 1 large bunch broccoli, chopped | ¼ cup low sodium soy sauce |
| 2 carrots, sliced | ½ cup umeboshi plum sauce |
| 4 large potatoes, chunked | 2 tsp. ground ginger root |
| 1 head cauliflower, chopped | 1 tsp. prepared horseradish |

Combine all ingredients in a large pot. Bring to a boil, reduce heat. Cover and cook until vegetables are tender, from 45-60 minutes. Before serving, thicken with a small amount of cornstarch or arrowroot mixed in cold water. Add cornstarch mixture to stew while stirring. Cook and stir until thickened.

Serve over rice or buckwheat soba noodles.

HELPFUL HINTS: See note on Plum Sauce under the heading Update on Ingredients (this volume).

*Contributed by Castle Medical Center Dietary Dept.*

## POI STEW

SERVINGS: 8

PREPARATION TIME: 30 mins.    COOKING TIME: 60 mins.

| | |
|---|---|
| 2 cups coarsely chopped onions | 1 bay leaf |
| 2 cups thickly sliced celery | ¼ tsp. garlic powder |
| 2 cups thickly sliced carrots | ⅛ tsp. basil |
| 2 cups peeled, cubed potatoes | ⅛ tsp. allspice |
| 2 cups water | ½ lb. poi |
| 2 tbsp. low sodium soy sauce | 1 cup peas |

Place onions, celery, carrots, and potatoes in a large pot with the water and the seasonings. Cook over medium heat until the vegetables are about half done, about 30 minutes. Add poi to thicken stew, stirring well. Add peas and mix in. Cook until all vegetables are tender, about 30 minutes longer.

HELPFUL HINTS: You may want to increase the amounts of seasoning used, especially the basil and allspice.

*Contributed by Janine Shrader*

### JANINES'S SPAGHETTI SAUCE

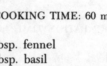

SERVINGS: 8-10

PREPARATION TIME: 15 mins.    COOKING TIME: 60 mins.

| | |
|---|---|
| 1 28 oz. can tomato puree | 1 tbsp. fennel |
| 1 12 oz. can tomato paste | 2 tbsp. basil |
| 5 cups water | 1 tbsp. honey |
| 2 large onions, diced | 1 tsp. oregano |
| 8-10 garlic cloves, crushed | black pepper to taste |

Place onions and garlic in a small amount of water in a large pot. Saute until soft, about 5 minutes. Add remaining ingredients and simmer uncovered for 1 hour or longer. Serve over pasta.

HELPFUL HINTS: Makes a large amount. Freezes well. Fennel seeds add a sausage-like flavor. Try them in many dishes.

### HAPOSAI
### (Japanese Vegetable Stew)

SERVINGS: 8

PREPARATION TIME: 30 mins.    COOKING TIME: 30 mins.

| | |
|---|---|
| 2 cups water | 2 green peppers, cut in 1 inch squares |
| ¼ cup low sodium soy sauce | 2 carrots, cut in ¼ inch slices |
| ¼ cup vinegar | 2 stalks celery, cut in ½ inch pieces |
| ¼ cup honey | 1 zucchini, cut in ½ inch slices |
| 2 tbsp. cornstarch or arrowroot | 1½ cups each cauliflower and broccoli pieces |
| 1 tsp. grated gingerroot | |
| 1 clove garlic, minced | |
| 2 16 oz. cans tomatoes | |
| 2 onions, cut in wedges | |

Combine first 7 ingredients in a large pot. Bring to a boil, stirring frequently until mixture thickens and clears. Add tomatoes, stir and remove from heat. Steam last 7 vegetables until tender, 20-30 minutes depending on how you like them. Add to sauce mixture. Heat through. Serve over brown rice.

HELPFUL HINTS: You may substitute or eliminate vegetables as desired. The only important vegetables are the tomatoes, onions and green peppers which are needed for flavor in this dish.

## GREEK STEW

SERVING: 6-8

PREPARATION TIME: 30 mins.    COOKING TIME: 3 hrs.

1 cup dried kidney beans
4 cups water
2 lbs. boiling onions, cleaned and
  left whole
2 cloves garlic, crushed
3 potatoes, chunked
2 carrots, sliced
1 leek, sliced
2 tbsp. lemon juice
3 cups cauliflower pieces

4 tomatoes, chunked
1 tsp. honey
2 tbsp. low sodium soy sauce
¾ tsp. cinnamon
2 tsp. ground cumin
Several dashes cayenne pepper
  (optional).
Several twists of fresh ground
  pepper (optional).

Place beans and water in a large pot. Cover and cook for 2 hours. Add onions, garlic, potatoes, carrots, leek and lemon juice. Cook for 30 minutes longer. Add remaining ingredients and cook an additional 30 minutes. Serve over brown rice or bulgur.

## SUMMER STEW

SERVINGS: 6-8

PREPARATION TIME: 30 mins.    COOKING TIME: 30 mins.

2 onions, sliced
2 cloves garlic, crushed
6 small zucchini, sliced ½ inch
  thick
4 small yellow crookneck squash,
  sliced ½ inch thick
1 green pepper, coarsely chopped

2 cups snow peas, trimmed and left
  whole
3 cups tomato chunks
2 cups corn kernels
3 tbsp. low sodium soy sauce
Seasonings (see note under hints).

Saute onions and garlic in ½ cup water in a large saucepan.
Cook until soft, about 5 minutes. Add both kinds of summer squash, green pepper, snow peas, and tomatoes, plus another ½ cup water. Cover and simmer over medium heat for 15-20 minutes. Stir occasionally. Add corn and chosen seasonings. Simmer an additional 10 minutes. Mix 1 tablespoon cornstarch or arrowroot in ¼ cup cold water. Gradually add to stew while stirring.
Cook and stir until thickened. Serve hot.

HELPFUL HINTS: This is a very low calorie stew (good for weight loss.) It is delicious with many different seasonings. Choose one of the four seasoning mixtures here, or use your own favorites.

1. 1 tsp. turmeric
   1½ tsp. ground cumin
   1 tsp. garam masala (recipe in Volume I)
   1 tbsp. chopped fresh coriander

2. 1 tsp. dried basil or 1 tbsp. fresh basil, chopped
   1 tsp. dried oregano or 1 tbsp. fresh oregano, chopped
   1 tbsp. parsley, chopped
   dash lemon juice

3. ½ tsp. basil
   1 tsp. dill weed
   1 tsp. paprika

4. ½ tsp. thyme
   ½ tsp. rosemary
   ½ tsp. marjoram
   ½ tbsp. Dijon mustard

# TEMPEH CREOLE

## SERVINGS: 8

PREPARATION TIME: 15 mins.    COOKING TIME: 35 mins.

2 onions, chopped
1 green pepper, chopped
½ cup celery, chopped
2 cloves garlic, crushed
1 (8 oz.) can tomato sauce
2 (15 oz.) cans tomatoes, chopped
2 bay leaves
1 tbsp. chopped parsley

1½ tbsp. natural Worcestershire sauce
1 tsp. chili powder
⅛ tsp. cayenne pepper
dash or two of Tabasco (optional)
8 oz. tempeh, cut into ½ inch pieces

Saute raw vegetables and garlic in ½ cup water for 5 minutes. Add remaining ingredients and simmer for 30 minutes, stirring occasionally. Serve over brown rice.

HELPFUL HINTS: To spice this up even more, try adding some of the Cajun Spices (recipe in this volume). Start with a small amount, taste and add more if desired. Tempeh is a cultured soy bean product. You can usually find it in natural food stores.

# QUICK SAUCY VEGETABLES

SERVINGS: 4

PREPARATION TIME: 10 mins.    COOKING TIME: 20 mins.

| | |
|---|---|
| 4 cups frozen vegetables | 2 tbsp. cornstarch or arrowroot |
| 2 cups water | Optional: Seasonings of your choice |
| 3 tbsp. low sodium soy sauce | (see helpful hints) |

Cook the vegetables in the water until tender, about 15 minutes. Add soy sauce and optional seasonings of your choice. Mix cornstarch or arrowroot in ¼ cup water. Add to vegetable mixture while stirring. Cook and stir until thickened. Serve over whole wheat toast for a quick, easy meal. Or serve over whole grains or pasta.

HELPFUL HINTS: This may also be made with assorted fresh vegetables. Keep the pieces small so they cook quickly. Optional choices for seasoning follow:
1. ½ tsp. turmeric
   ½ tsp. ground cumin
   ½ tsp. garam masala (recipe in Volume I)

2. ½ tsp. basil
   ½ tsp. dill weed
   ½ tsp. paprika

3. ½ tsp. thyme
   ½ tsp. rosemary
   ½ tsp. marjoram

# JEWISH YAM STEW

SERVINGS: 8

PREPARATION TIME: 30 mins.    COOKING TIME: 1 hr.

¾ cup dried apricots
¾ cup pitted prunes
2 cups hot water
1 large yam, peeled and cut into cubes
3 large sweet potatoes, peeled and cut into cubes

2 carrots, sliced
1 apple, chopped
¾ cup orange juice
1 tbsp. lemon juice
½ tsp. cinnamom
pinch of ground cloves
2 tbsp. honey

Soak apricots and prunes in the hot water for 30 minutes.

Meanwhile, place yams, sweet potatoes, and carrots in large sauce pan. Add 1 cup water, bring to boil, cover, reduce heat to medium and cook for 30 minutes. Add the remaining ingredients. Drain the apricots and prunes and add them to the potato mixture. Mix well and pour into a casserole dish. Bake, covered, in a 350 degree oven for 1 hour. Serve hot or cold.

HELPFUL HINTS: May be prepared ahead, up to the baking time. Cover and refrigerate until ready to bake. Add 15 minutes to baking time.

## MOROCCAN STEW

SERVINGS: 6

PREPARATION TIME: 30 mins.    COOKING TIME: 60 mins.
(cooked beans needed)

1 cup water
1 onion, chopped
2 green peppers, chopped
1½ tsp. ground coriander
¾ tsp. ground cinnamon
½ tsp. ground cumin
2 sweet potatoes, peeled and cut into ½ inch cubes

2 tomatoes, chopped
1 tbsp. lemon juice
1 tbsp. low sodium soy sauce
2 tsp. pure prepared horseradish
¼ tsp. Tabasco
⅛ tsp. saffron
2 cups cooked garbanzos
2 zucchini, chopped

In a large pan, saute the onion, green pepper, coriander, cinnamon and cumin in ½ cup water for 5 minutes. Add the sweet potatoes and cook and stir for a few minutes. Then add tomatoes, lemon juice, soy sauce, horseradish, saffron, Tabasco and the garbanzos along with the remaining ½ cup water. Bring to a boil, reduce heat, cover and cook for 30 minutes. Add zucchini, mix well and continue to cook an additional 15 minutes.

Serve over bulgur wheat with Sweet and Sour Fruit Sauce (recipe in this volume) to spoon over the top.

# CREAMED CURRIED VEGETABLES

SERVINGS: 4-6

PREPARATION TIME: 20 mins.    COOKING TIME: 30 mins.

2 onions, sliced
½ lb. mushrooms, sliced
1 green pepper, chopped
1 cup cut green beans
1 cup green peas (frozen)
2 small zucchini, sliced
1 tsp. turmeric
1 tsp. ground cumin

1 tsp. ground coriander
1 tsp. garam masala (recipe in Vol. I)
⅛ tsp. pepper (optional)
2 tbsp. low sodium soy sauce
2 cups water
2 cups nut milk, rice milk or oat milk

In a large saucepan, saute the onions, mushrooms and green pepper in ½ cup water for 5 minutes. Add remaining vegetables, saute for 5 minutes more. Add the spices, mix well, then add remaining water, acceptable milk and soy sauce. Bring to a boil, reduce heat slightly and cook about 20 minutes, stirring occasionally. Before serving, mix 1-2 tbsp. cornstarch into ¼ cup cold water, add to curry mixture while stirring. Cook and stir until thickened. Serve over whole wheat or rye toast; or over whole grains or potatoes.

# MULTI GRAIN STEW

SERVINGS: 8

PREPARATION TIME: 20 mins.    COOKING TIME: 3 hrs.

½ cup whole rye
½ cup whole wheat berries
½ cup barley
½ cup millet
8 cups water
1 large onion, chopped
2 stalks celery, sliced
2 carrots, thickly sliced
2 leeks, sliced

1 large sweet potato, coarsely chopped
1 clove garlic, minced
1 16 oz. can tomatoes with liquid
½ cup chopped parsley
2 tbsp. low sodium soy sauce
1 tsp. paprika
1 tsp. basil
½ tsp. ground cumin

Optional Spices:

¼ tsp. white pepper

½ tsp. Tabasco Sauce

Place all ingredients in a large pot. Bring to boil, reduce heat, cover, and simmer for 3 hours. Stir occasionally. This is quite spicy with the optional ingredients. Omit or reduce the pepper and Tabasco for milder stew.

HELPFUL HINTS: This may also be made in a slow cooker. It will take about 8 hours on the high temperature setting.

*Contributed by Ann Tang*

## ANN'S SUPER CURRY

SERVINGS: 3-4

PREPARATION TIME: 20 mins.    COOKING TIME: 1¼ hrs.

1 onion, chopped
2 carrots, sliced
1 green pepper, chopped
1 stalk celery, chopped
6-8 fresh mushrooms, sliced
½ cup frozen peas (optional)
1 large taro, chunked (or 2 potatoes)
2-3 cloves garlic, minced
1 tbsp. curry powder
1-2 tsp. crushed coriander seeds

1 tsp. turmeric
1 tsp. cumin
¼ tsp. dry mustard
¼ tsp. anise seeds
¼ tsp. crushed red chili pepper (optional)
dash: nutmeg
cinnamon
powdered ginger
cayenne

Saute onions and garlic in a small amount of water until transparant. Add carrots, green pepper, celery and curry powder. Saute for a few more minutes. Add the rest of the seasonings and simmer for 15 minutes. Add taro (or potatoes) and enough water to cover. Continue cooking until taro (or potatoes) are tender (about 40 minutes.) Add mushrooms and peas. Cook 10 minutes longer.

Serve with brown rice, in a pita bread or in chapati.

HELPFUL HINTS: Freezes well.

## CAJUN BEAN STEW

SERVINGS: 8

PREPARATION TIME: 30 mins.    COOKING TIME: 2½ hrs.

1 lb. dried black-eyed peas
1 cup dried lima beans
8 cups water
2 cups corn (frozen)
2 cups okra (frozen)
1 sweet potato, sliced

Several dashes of Louisiana Hot
  Sauce
1½ tsp. Cajun spices
  (recipe in this book)
4 cups shredded greens
  (kale, mustard greens,
  spinach, swiss chard, etc.)

Place black-eyed peas and lima beans in a large pot with 8 cups of water. Bring to a boil, reduce heat, cover and cook for 1½ hours. Add corn, okra(cut in pieces, if desired), sweet potato, onion, and seasonings. Cover and cook an additional 30 minutes. Add greens and cook about 30 minutes.

HELPFUL HINTS: Pass the Louisiana Hot Sauce at the table to shake on individual servings, if desired.

# Main Dishes

## Beans

### SPICY LENTIL FILLING

SERVINGS: 8-10

PREPARATION TIME: 15 mins.    COOKING TIME: 1½ hrs.

2 onions, chopped
2 cloves garlic, pressed
3 tomatoes, chopped
1½ tbsp. curry powder

¼ tsp. cayenne (optional)
1½ cups lentils
5 ½ cups water
2 tbsp. low sodium soy sauce

Place ½ cup water in a large saucepan. Add onion and garlic, cook, stirring frequently until softened, about 5 minutes. Add tomatoes, curry powder and cayenne. Continue to cook until tomato softens, about 5 more minutes. Add the remaining water, lentils and soy sauce. Bring to a boil, reduce heat, cover and cook for 30 minutes. Uncover, cook, stirring often for an additional 45 minutes, stirring frequently until thickened somewhat.

To serve hot, fill chapatis or pita bread, or corn tortillas with some of the mixture. Garnish with chopped tomatoes, green onions, cucumber, fresh coriander and your favorite salsa.

HELPFUL HINTS: This also makes a wonderful sandwich spread when cold. Keeps several days in the refrigerator. Also freezes well. This is a meal that could easily be prepared over the weekend, refrigerated and then heated up for a fast meal during the week.

# FALAFEL

SERVINGS: 15 patties

PREPARATION TIME: 45 mins.    COOKING TIME: 15-30 mins.
(cooked beans needed)

½ cup raw bulgur
5 cups cooked garbanzo beans
3 cloves garlic, pressed
3 tbsp. tahini
3 tbsp. whole wheat flour
2 tbsp. low sodium soy sauce
1 tsp. ground cumin

1 tsp. ground coriander
1 tsp. turmeric
⅛ to ¼ tsp. cayenne
⅓ cup water
4 tbsp. chopped fresh coriander or
    parsley

Pour 2 cups boiling water over the bulgur in a bowl. Let sit for 20 minutes. Meanwhile, combine garbanzos and remaining ingredients (except the fresh coriander) in the bowl of a food processor. Process until well mixed. (If you do not have a food processor, see under HELPFUL HINTS on what to use instead.) Drain bulgur in a strainer, press against the sides to remove water. Combine bulgur, garbanzo mixture and fresh coriander or parsley. Shape into patties. Cook by either (1) or (2) method.

(1) Place patties on a non-stick baking sheet. Bake at 350 degrees for 15 minutes. Turn over and bake an additional 15 minutes.

(2) Place on a non-stick griddle. Cook over medium heat about 7-8 minutes on each side.

Serve in pita bread, garnished with tomatoes, cucumbers, lettuce and tahini sauce (recipe elsewhere in book).

HELPFUL HINTS: If you do not have a food processor, a blender can be used if you do it in several batches. Or finely mash the beans, then mix in the remaining ingredients. Can be frozen.

Also as an option, you may want to add 2 tsp. egg replacer mixed in 4 tbsp. water to help hold them together. Add to the final mixture, just before shaping into patties.

# PASTA E FAGIOLI

SERVINGS: 6-8

PREPARATION TIME: 30 mins.    COOKING TIME: 2 hrs.

1½ cups dried white beans
4 cups water
1 onion, chopped
2 stalks celery, sliced
2 carrots, sliced
2 cloves garlic, pressed

1 can (16 oz.) chopped tomatoes
  with juice
1 bay leaf
1 tsp. oregano
½ tsp. basil
2 cups uncooked pasta (shells,
  elbows, corkscrew, etc.)
chopped fresh parsley

Place beans and water in a large pot. Soak overnight OR bring to a boil, boil one minute, remove from heat, cover and let rest 1 hour.

Then add onion, celery, carrots, garlic, tomatoes, and herbs. Bring to a boil. Reduce heat, cover and cook over medium-low heat for 1-2 hours, until beans and vegetables are soft. (Cooking time will vary depending on how you soaked the beans.)

About 30 minutes before serving, cook the pasta in boiling water until tender. Drain, rinse under cool water. Add pasta to bean mixture. Heat for about 5-10 minutes. Add some fresh ground black pepper, if desired. Garnish with chopped parsley just before serving.

## MILTON'S SPECIAL BARBEQUE

SERVINGS: makes about 7 cups

PREPARATION TIME: 30 mins.    COOKING TIME: 30 mins.

3 cups crumbled tofu (30 oz.)
2 tbsp. low sodium soy sauce
1 tbsp. tomato paste
1 tbsp. peanut butter
1 tsp. onion powder
⅛ tsp. garlic powder

¼ cup water
1 onion, chopped
1 green pepper, chopped
1-2 cloves garlic, pressed
1 pkg. (10 oz.) Nature's Burger Mix
4 cups barbeque sauce (recipe in
  this book)

Mix the soy sauce, tomato paste, peanut butter, onion powder and garlic powder together until they are smooth. Add the ¼ cup water and mix well. Pour over the crumbled tofu and stir until the tofu is coated with the mixture.

Saute the onion, green pepper and garlic in ½ cup water until soft. Add tofu mixture and continue to cook and stir about 5 minutes to absorb some of the liquid.

Add the Nature's Burger Mix and the barbeque sauce. Mix well. Cook over low heat for 20 minutes, stirring occasionally.

Serve on whole wheat buns or whole wheat bread.

HELPFUL HINTS: This makes a large amount of barbeque. It freezes well so it's easy to divide into small portions to use for another meal.

# FRESH VEGETABLE CHILI

SERVINGS: 6

PREPARATION TIME: 30 mins.    COOKING TIME: 30 mins.
(cooked beans needed)

| | |
|---|---|
| 1 cup water | 4 medium to large tomatoes, chopped |
| 2 onions, chopped | |
| ½ lb. mushrooms, sliced | 2 cups broccoli florets |
| 1 green pepper, chopped | 2 tbsp. chili powder |
| 2 smallish zucchini, cut in half, then sliced | 3 cups cooked kidney beans |
| | 2 tbsp. cornstarch or arrowroot mixed in ⅓ cup water |

Place ½ cup water in a large pot. Add onions and saute over medium-high heat for 3 minutes. Add mushrooms, green pepper, zucchini, tomatoes, broccoli, chili powder and remaining ½ cup water. Cover and bring to a boil. Reduce heat to medium. Cook for 10 minutes, stirring occasionally. Add beans. Heat through, about 5 minutes. Add cornstarch mixture to the vegetables while stirring. Cook and stir until thickened. Serve over brown rice. Pass optional toppings to spoon over the top, if desired.

TOPPINGS (optional):

1. 1 bunch green onions, finely chopped
2. chopped cucumbers
3. sliced radishes
4. diced canned green chilies
5. sliced black olives
6. chopped fresh coriander

Use as many or as few as you choose.

HELPFUL HINTS: A wonderful meal to prepare when you have lots of fresh garden vegetables to use up.

## MULTIPLE BEAN CASSEROLE

SERVINGS: 8

PREPARATION TIME: 30 mins.     COOKING TIME: 2½ hrs.
(less if using cooked beans)

1 cup dried kidney beans
1 cup dried lima beans
1 cup dried black-eyed peas
1 dried black beans
1 onion, chopped
1 clove garlic, crushed
2¼ cups water
½ cup bulgur

½ cup acceptable ketchup
(or tomato puree)
¼ cup red wine (or apple juice)
¼ cup honey
2 tbsp. prepared mustard
1 tsp. ground cumin
1 tbsp. low sodium soy sauce

Place beans in a large pot, cover with plenty of water, cook until just tender, approx. 1½ hours. Drain. Place beans in a 4 qt. casserole dish. Set aside. (If you have cooked beans on hand, use a total of about 8 cups cooked beans.)

In a saucepan, saute the onion and garlic in ¼ cup water for 5 minutes. Add the remaining ingredients, mix well. Pour over beans in casserole dish. Mix well. Cover. Bake at 325 degrees for 1 hour.

HELPFUL HINTS: This dish can be put together very quickly if you have some cooked beans on hand. It can also be prepared ahead and kept in the refrigerator until the final baking.

## SOUTHERN STYLE BLACK EYED PEAS

SERVINGS: 4-6

PREPARATION TIME: 45 mins.     COOKING TIME: 1½ hrs.

2½ cups black eyed peas
5 cups water
1 large onion, chopped
1 clove garlic, crushed

½ tsp. crushed red pepper
1 tbsp. low sodium soy sauce
¾ tsp. Tabasco sauce

ONIONS:

2 medium onions, thinly sliced
2 tbsp. lemon juice

½ tsp. Tabasco sauce

GREENS:

1 medium onion, chopped
10 cups finely chopped leafy greens
(2 large bunches) (mustard greens,
    kale, chard, etc.)

SALSA:

1 cup of your favorite salsa

GARNISHES:

1 cup of chopped green onions

Place black eyed peas and water in a medium sauce pot. Bring to a boil, reduce heat, cover and cook for 30 minutes. Add chopped onion, garlic and seasonings. Cook an additional 60 minutes. Serve plain or over brown rice.

ONIONS: Place onions in a pan with about ½ cup water. Saute over medium heat until limp. Transfer to a bowl. Add remaining ingredients. Mix. Cover and refrigerate at least 1 hour to blend flavors.

GREENS: Rinse greens and drain. Finely chop the greens (use a food processor if you have one) and the onion. (Save in a plastic bag until just before serving.) Place a small amount of water in a pan. Add greens and onion and saute until just wilted. Then cover and steam about 10 minutes. Drain. Sprinkle with some fresh lemon juice.

HELPFUL HINTS: This is another "fun meal", many layers to choose from. Place some brown rice on your plate, ladle some black eyed peas over that. Then follow with some marinated onions, steamed greens, salsa and green onions. Use as many or as few as you choose. This is also delicious in chapati or pita bread instead of over brown rice. Use the same toppings.

## BLACK BEANS AND NECTARINES

### SERVINGS: 6-8

PREPARATION TIME: 20 mins.    COOKING TIME: 3 hrs.

2½ cups black beans
7 ½ cups water
2 onions, chopped
5 medium nectarines, peeled and
    chopped
1 (15 oz) can tomato sauce

2 cloves garlic, pressed
⅛ cup honey
1 tbsp. chili powder
1 tsp. dry mustard
¼ cup uncooked millet

Place beans and water in a large pot. Soak overnight OR bring to a boil, boil for 1-2 minutes, remove from heat and let rest for 1 hour. Then add onions, bring to boil again, reduce heat and simmer, covered for 2 hours. Add remaining ingredients and cook an additional 45-60 minutes over low heat. Serve in large bowls topped with your choice of chopped green onions, chopped cucumber, or snipped parsley.

HELPFUL HINTS: May also be served over potatoes, sweet potatoes, whole grains or noodles.

*Contributed by Shannon McMonagle*

## FALAFELS

SERVINGS: 4-6

PREPARATION TIME: 30 mins.    COOKING TIME: 20-25 mins.
(cooked beans and potato needed)

2 cups cooked, pureed, garbanzos
1 potato, baked, peeled and mashed
3 tbsp. tahini
1 small bunch Chinese parsley, minced
1/2 onion, minced
1/8 tsp. garlic powder

1/8 tsp. black pepper
1 tsp. paprika
1/8 cup sesame seeds
1/8 cup sunflower seeds
squirt of fresh lemon

In a large bowl, mix the beans, potato and tahini. Add the remaining ingredients and mix well. Drop by spoonfuls on a non-stick baking sheet and bake at 350 degrees for 20-25 minutes.

Serve stuffed inside a pita bread with fresh vegetables and topped with Tahini Sauce or Salsa.

## BOSTON BAKED BEANS

SERVINGS: 4-6

PREPARATION TIME: 15 mins.    COOKING TIME: 20 mins.
(cooked beans needed)

1 medium onion, chopped
1 16 oz. can tomatoes, chopped
2 tbsp. maple syrup
1 tbsp. vinegar
1 tbsp. low sodium soy sauce
1 tbsp. parsley flakes

1 1/2 tsp. dry mustard
1 1/4 tsp. powdered ginger
1/2 tsp. ground cinnamon
1/4 tsp. black pepper
5 cups cooked white beans

Saute the onion in a small amount of water until soft. Add remaining ingredients, except for the beans. Cook and stir about 5 minutes. Add beans, cook about 10-15 minutes to blend flavors.

*Contributed by Linda DuPuy*

## BEAN AND VEGETABLE CASSEROLE

SERVINGS: 8-10

PREPARATION TIME: 35 mins.    COOKING TIME: 60 mins.
(cooked beans needed)

4 cups cooked white beans
1 head cauliflower, chopped
6 cups chopped tomato
4 cups chopped broccoli
3 medium onions, chopped
2 cups chopped celery
1 cup sliced carrots
3 tbsp. molasses

3 tbsp. low sodium soy sauce
1 tbsp. chili powder
1 tbsp. basil
½ to 1½ tsp. cayenne
(use the smaller amount if you
don't like things too hot—
increase amount for more
hotness).

Place beans in a large casserole. Add remaining ingredients and mix well. Bake, covered, at 350 degrees for 1 hour. Serve plain or on corn or flour tortillas.

## SIX-WAY-FUN CHILI

SERVINGS: 8

PREPARATION TIME: 45 mins.    COOKING TIME: 3-4 hrs.

6 cups water
2½ cups dried kidney beans
4 onions, chopped
1 green pepper, chopped
2 stalks celery, sliced
1 (16 oz.) can tomatoes with juice,
chopped up
1 (6 oz.) can tomato paste

1½ tbsp. chili powder
1 tsp. cumin
1 tsp. carob powder
¼ tsp. cinnamon
¼ tsp. ground coriander
¼ tsp. ground mustard
¼ tsp. ground cardamom

Place the water and beans in a large saucepot. Soak overnight, or bring to boil, boil 1 minute, remove from heat and let rest 1 hour. Bring beans and water to a boil again. Cook for 1 hour, then add onions, green pepper, celery, tomatoes and tomato paste. Stir to mix well. Cover and continue to cook over medium-low heat for 15 minutes. Then stir in spices. Cover and continue to cook until beans are tender, 2 to 3 hours. Serve in large bowls.

Place the following six toppings in individual serving dishes. Pass these at the table to layer on the chili in any order desired.

1. MARINATED ONIONS:

1½ tbsp. vinegar
1 large red onion, sliced
2 tsp. vinegar

1 tbsp. water
½ tsp. mustard seeds
½ tsp. cumin seeds

Place 2 cups water and 1½ tbsp. vinegar in a saucepan. Bring to a boil. Add onions, cook 2 minutes, drain. Combine with remaining ingredients. Refrigerate to blend flavors.

2. GREEN ONIONS:

1 bunch green onions, including
   tops, finely chopped

3. TOMATOES:

2-3 tomatoes, chopped

4. GREEN CHILES:

1 can diced green chilies

5. CUCUMBER:

1 cucumber, peeled and chopped

6. GREENS:

1 onion, chopped

10 cups finely chopped leafy greens
   (2 bunches)

Saute onion and greens in a small amount of water for a few minutes. Then cover and steam for about 10-15 minutes. Drain.

HELPFUL HINTS: This may also be made in a slow cooker. Add all chili ingredients at once. Cook on high for 6-8 hours.

The term "fun chili" comes from my daughter, Heather, who likes meals with lots of layers. She calls them "fun meals".

This may also be served over rice or another grain.

# SOUTH AMERICAN BEAN STEW

SERVINGS: 8-10

PREPARATION TIME: 45 mins.     COOKING TIME: 3 hrs.

STEW:

1 cup dried pink beans
1¼ cups dried white beans
6 cups water
3 large onions, chopped
2 cloves garlic, crushed
2 (16 oz.) cans chopped tomatoes,
  drained

1½ tsp. basil
1½ tsp. oregano
4 cups chopped winter squash
2 cups corn kernels

SPICY SAUCE:

1 onion, chopped
1 clove garlic, pressed
½ tsp. dried crushed red pepper

1 cup water
¾ cup chopped fresh coriander
  leaves
1½ tbsp. wine vinegar

STEW: Place beans in a large soup pot with the water. Bring to a boil, turn off heat, let rest for 1 hour.

Bring to a boil again, cover, reduce heat and cook for 1 hour. Meanwhile, saute onions and garlic in ¼ cup of water for 5 minutes, stirring often. Add chopped tomatoes, basil, and oregano. Simmer over low heat about 20 minutes.

Add tomato mixture to beans. Add squash pieces. Cover and simmer for 45 minutes. Add corn kernels. Cook an additional 15 minutes. Serve over rice. Spoon some spicy sauce over the top if desired.

SPICY SAUCE: Saute onion, garlic and pepper in ¼ cup of water until very soft. Remove from heat. Add remaining ingredients. Mix well. Refrigerate at least 1 hour to blend flavors.

# FEJOIADA

SERVINGS: 6-8

PREPARATION TIME: 1½ hrs.     COOKING TIME: 3 hrs.

**BEANS:**

2½ cups dried black beans
5 cups water
1 large onion, chopped
2 stalks celery, chopped

2 cloves garlic, pressed
1 bay leaf
½ tsp. crushed red pepper
2 medium tomatoes, chopped

**RICE:**

2½ cups raw brown rice
3 cups water

2 cups tomato juice

**ONIONS:**

2 onions, thinly sliced
2 tbsp. lemon juice

½ tsp. Tabasco Sauce

**GREENS:**

1 onion, chopped
10 cups finely chopped greens
  (collard greens, Kale, romaine,
  chard)—
  2 large bunches

**SALSA:**

1 (16 oz.) can tomatoes, drained
¼ cup canned green chilies
½ small onion, chopped

2 tbsp. vinegar
1 tbsp. lemon juice
¼ tsp. Tabasco

**GARNISH:**

Peeled, sliced oranges

Place the beans and the water in a large pot. Soak overnight, or bring to a boil, boil 1 minute, remove from heat and let "rest" for 1 hour. Then bring to boil, reduce heat, cover and simmer for 1 hour. Then add onions, celery, garlic, bay leaf and crushed pepper. Continue to cook until beans are almost tender, about 1½ hours. Add tomatoes and cook an additional ½ hour.

While beans are cooking, place onions in a sauce pan with about ½ cup water. Saute over medium heat until limp. Transfer to bowl. Add lemon juice and Tabasco. Mix well. Cover and refrigerate at least 1 hour to blend flavors.

Rinse greens and drain. Finely chop greens and the onion (use a food processor, if you have one.) Reserve in a plastic bag until just before serving. Then place a small amount of water in a pan, add greens and onion, and saute until just wilted. Then cover and steam about 10 minutes. Drain. Place in serving bowl. Sprinkle with some fresh lemon juice.

Begin cooking the rice about 1 hour before dinner. Place water and juice in a saucepan. Bring to a boil. Add rice, cover and simmer over low heat for 45 minutes. Remove from heat and let rest for 15 minutes before serving.

To prepare salsa, place all ingredients in a blender jar. Blend until smooth. Refrigerate until serving time.

When ready to serve, place all ingredients in serving bowls. To assemble, place rice on plate first, cover with the black beans, then layer on the orange slices, the greens, the spicy onions and the salsa. Each person adds as much of the extras or as little as they wish.

HELPFUL HINTS: This is a native dish of Brazil, adapted from ideas my in-laws brought back after living there for a year. Makes an interesting buffet dinner to share with friends.

## *Contributed by Ann Tang*
## QUICK CHILI

SERVINGS: 4-6

PREPARATION TIME: 15 mins.   COOKING TIME: 30 mins.
(cooked beans needed)

½ cup water
2 onions, chopped
1 green pepper, chopped
1 stalk celery, chopped
1 clove garlic, crushed

2 (16 oz.) cans tomatoes, cut-up
4 cups cooked kidney beans
2 tbsp. chili powder
2 tsp. ground cumin

Place water, onions, green pepper, celery, and garlic in a medium sauce pan and saute over high heat for 3-4 minutes. Add remaining ingredients, bring to a boil, reduce heat and cook gently for another 25 minutes or so to blend flavors. Stir occasionally.

HELPFUL HINTS: Serve over brown rice or baked potatoes, or scoop into a large bowl. Garnish with chopped onions, diced green chilis, shredded greens, or other of your favorite additions for chili. Fresh tomatoes may be used instead of the canned. Other beans may be used instead of the Kidney beans, such as black beans or white beans.

# BARBEQUED BURGERS

SERVINGS: 10 burgers

PREPARATION TIME: 15 mins.

PRECOOKING TIME: 45 mins.
COOLING TIME: 1 hr.
COOKING TIME: 15 mins.

1 cup lentils
3 cups water
1 onion, finely chopped
1 clove garlic, crushed
1 stalk celery, finely chopped

1 carrot grated
½ cup bulgur wheat
2 tbsp. Ketchup sauce or tomato
  sauce
1 tsp. prepared mustard
1 tsp. chili powder

Place lentils and water in a medium sauce pan. Bring to a boil, add onions, garlic, celery and carrot. Reduce heat, cover and simmer for 30 minutes. Add remaining ingredients. Cook an additional 15 minutes. Remove from heat and let cool. Shape into patties and cook on a non-stick griddle until browned, about 15 minutes. Serve in a whole wheat bun with a variety of favorite condiments.

HELPFUL HINTS: Make ahead, then broil just before dinner. These may also be baked on a non-stick baking sheet. Bake at 350 degrees for 15 minutes on each side.

*Contributed by Castle Medical Center Dietary Dept.*

## MUNGO BEANS

SERVINGS: 8

PREPARATION TIME: 20 mins.

COOKING TIME: 1½ hrs.

2 cups dried whole mung beans
1 cup onions, sliced
1 pkg. Shiitaki mushrooms (1 oz.)
4 cups sliced fresh tomatoes

1 clove garlic, minced
½ tsp. minced fresh gingerroot
2 tbsp. low sodium soy sauce

Wash beans well and drain. Place in a large pot. Add enough water to cover beans and cook for 1 hour. Meanwhile, soak mushrooms in hot water until soft, drain, squeeze out water and slice.

Saute onions, mushrooms, tomatoes, garlic and ginger in a small amount of water for 5 minutes. Add to mung beans, mix well, add soy sauce and continue to cook about 30 minutes longer until beans are tender.

*Contributed by Judi Smith*

# BEAN LOAF

SERVINGS: 8

PREPARATION TIME: 30 mins.    COOKING TIME: 45 mins.
(cooked beans and rice needed)

5 cups cooked beans (any kind)
1 cup cooked brown rice
1 onion, chopped
1 green pepper, chopped
1 cup chopped, celery
1 clove garlic, crushed
1 ½ cups tomato sauce
1 cup bread crumbs
2 tbsp. bran

1 tsp. basil
1 tsp. oregano
2 tsp. chili powder
1 tsp. cumin
⅛ tsp. cayenne (optional)
1 tbsp. parsley flakes
1 tbsp. low sodium soy sauce
  (optional)
2 tbsp. corn meal

Mash the beans and combine them with the rice. Set aside. Saute the onion, green pepper, celery and garlic in ⅓ cup water for 5 minutes. Add to the bean-rice mixture. Add all of the remaining ingredients, except the corn meal, and mix well.

Sprinkle the corn meal over the bottom of a 9″ × 5″ × 3″ non-stick loaf pan. Place the bean mixture in the pan, smoothing out the top. Bake at 350 degrees for 45 minutes.

HELPFUL HINTS: Makes a delicious sandwich spread when cold.

# SPICY MIXED BEAN CHILI

SERVINGS: 4

PREPARATION TIME: 20 mins.    COOKING TIME: 4 hrs.

½ cup black beans
½ cup pink beans
½ cup pinto beans
4 cups water
1 onion, chopped
2 cloves garlic, pressed

1 (16 oz.) can chopped tomatoes
¼ cup chopped canned green
  chilies
2 tbsp. chili powder
1 tsp. ground cumin
1/16 tsp. cayenne (optional)

GARNISHES: Chopped green onions, chopped fresh coriander, chopped tomatoes, chopped cucumber.

Place beans and water in a medium pot. Bring to a boil, boil for 2 minutes, remove from heat and let rest for 1 hour. Return to heat, add onions and garlic, bring to a boil, reduce heat to medium, cover and cook for 1 hour. Add remaining ingredients, except for garnishes, continue to cook for another 2 hours until beans are tender. Serve in bowls or over brown rice or potatoes. Pass garnishes to spoon over top as desired.

HELPFUL HINTS: May be made in a slow cooker. Add all ingredients at once (except garnishes) and cook on high for 8-10 hours.

## FLAVORFUL "REFRIED" BEANS

### SERVINGS: 8-12

### PREPARATION TIME: 5 mins.   COOKING TIME: 20 mins.
(cooked beans needed)

6 cups cooked pinto beans
½-1 cup bean cooking liquid (or water)
½ tsp. ground cumin

½ tsp. onion powder
½ tsp. chili powder
½ cup picante sauce or mild salsa

Mash the cooked pinto beans with a small amount of the cooking liquid (or water). Add cumin, onion powder and chili powder. Stir in the salsa of your choice, either mild or spicy. Cook over low heat until heated through. Serve on tostados, chapatis, in pita bread, or in bean enchiladas.

## BLACK BEAN CHILI

### SERVINGS: 8

### PREPARATION TIME: 30 mins.   COOKING TIME: 4 hrs.

3 cups black beans
7 cups water
2 onions, coarsely chopped
2 cloves garlic, pressed
¼ cup chopped canned green chilies
1 16 oz. can tomatoes, chopped (including liquid)

2 tsp. ground cumin
1 tsp. ground coriander
2 tsp. chili powder
⅛ tsp. cayenne
½ tsp. Tabasco
1 tbsp. tequila (entirely optional)
¼ cup chopped, fresh coriander

GARNISHES:
lime wedges, chopped green onions, sliced radishes, chopped tomatoes, chopped black olives or chopped cucumbers.

Place beans and water in a large pot. Bring to boil and cook for 2 minutes, remove from heat and let rest 1 hour.

Bring to boil again, reduce heat, cover and simmer for 1½ hours. Add onions, garlic, chilies, tomatoes, cumin, coriander, chili powder, Tabasco and cayenne. Continue to cook an additional 2½ hours.

Stir in tequila (an entirely optional ingredient) and fresh coriander before serving.

Serve in individual bowls or over brown rice. Pass garnishes to spoon over the top of the chili, if desired.

HELPFUL HINTS: Because this takes so long to cook, I recommend that you make it in a slow cooker—add all ingredients except tequila and coriander. Cook on high about 10 hours. OR soak beans overnight to reduce cooking time.

# Main Dishes
# Rice and Grains

## SPICY CHINESE RICE

SERVINGS: 6

PREPARATION TIME: 30 mins.     COOKING TIME: 20 mins.
(cooked rice needed)

4 tbsp. low sodium soy sauce
2 tbsp. cider vinegar
2 cloves garlic, crushed
2 tsp. grated fresh gingerroot
¼ tsp. crushed red pepper
1 onion, cut in half and sliced
½ lb. mushrooms, sliced
1½ cups chopped broccoli

2 cups chopped Chinese cabbage
1 cup bean sprouts
2 cups optional sliced vegetable (asparagus, snow peas, celery, carrots, green onions, etc.)
4 cups cooked brown rice
1 tbsp. low sodium soy sauce (optional)
3-4 tbsp. chopped fresh coriander

Place first 5 ingredients in a wok or large pot. Bring to a boil. Add vegetables in batches (see HELPFUL HINTS) and cook and stir over medium-high heat until crisp-tender (about 10-15 minutes depending on the size of the vegetable pieces). Add the cooked rice, the soy sauce and the coriander. Cook and stir until heated through. Serve at once.

HELPFUL HINTS: This can easily be made in small amounts to serve less people. It does keep well, and can even be frozen. Other combinations of vegetables may also be used. Keep the pieces small so they cook quickly. When adding the vegetables, do it in batches to give each vegetable a chance to get coated with the liquid. Begin with the onions and mushrooms, cook and stir for a minute, add the broccoli and optional vegetables, cook for a minute, then add the remaining vegetables and proceed as directed. This is an optional procedure but I find it makes for very flavorful vegetables.

## MEXICAN RICE

### SERVINGS: 6

PREPARATION TIME: 20 mins.    COOKING TIME: 20 mins.
(cooked rice needed)

5 cups cooked brown rice
1 onion, chopped
1 green pepper, chopped
1 bunch green onions, chopped
½ lb. mushrooms, sliced
2 cloves garlic, crushed
¼ cup chopped green chilies
1 (1 lb.) can tomatoes, chopped
   (add liquid also)

1 (2.2 oz.) can sliced black olives
   (drained)—(optional)
1 can water packed artichoke
   hearts, drained
1 cup cooked corn kernels
¼ cup chopped fresh coriander
2 tsp. chili powder
1 tsp. ground cumin
dash of Tabasco sauce

Using a large pot, saute the onion, green pepper, green onions, and garlic in ¼ cup water for 5 minutes. Add the mushrooms and saute 5 minutes longer. Add the remaining ingredients. Mix well. Cook over medium low heat about 10 minutes until heated through. Stir occasionally. Serve with salsa to spoon over the top, if desired.

*Contributed by Janine Shrader*
## WILD RICE CASSEROLE

### SERVINGS: 8

PREPARATION TIME: 40 mins.    COOKING TIME: 30 mins.

1 (8 oz.) pkg. wild rice
2 carrots, sliced
3 potatoes, peeled and diced
1 (10 oz.) basket pearl onions,
   cleaned and left whole

2 zucchini, chopped
½ lb. mushrooms, quartered
2 cups sauce, such as: Almond
   Sauce, Dill Sauce, Nutty
   Sauce, or one of your favorites

Prepare wild rice according to package directions. Prepare vegetables as directed and steam until tender. Prepare sauce of your choice.

In a large casserole combine wild rice and vegetables. Add sauce and mix gently. Bake at 350 degrees for 30 minutes.

## LUAU RICE

SERVINGS: 8

PREPARATION TIME: 15 mins.    COOKING TIME: 60 mins.

1 onion, chopped
1 clove garlic, minced
1 tbsp. curry powder
1½ cups long grain brown rice

3 ¼ cups water
dash white pepper
2 tomatoes, chopped
1 bunch finely chopped green
  onions

In a medium saucepan, saute the onion and garlic in ¼ cup water about 5 minutes. Add curry powder, rice, white pepper and remaining water. Bring to boil, reduce heat to low, cover and simmer for 45 minutes. Remove from heat. Let stand for 15 minutes without stirring. Add tomatoes and green onions, toss gently before serving. May be served hot or cold.

*Contributed by L. C. Gough*

## QUICK RICE DINNER

SERVINGS: 2

PREPARATION TIME: 10 mins.    COOKING TIME: 10-15 mins.
(cooked rice needed)

1 medium onion, sliced
3 whole cloves
1 to 2 inch piece of stick
  cinnamon, broken
generous grinding of
  black peppercorns

2 cups cooked brown rice
½ cup frozen peas, thawed
2 tomatoes, cut into wedges

Saute onion and spices in ¼ cup water until onions are cooked but still crisp, about 3 minutes. Add brown rice, stirring gently and heat through. Add peas, heat a few minutes. Serve with tomato wedges.

*Contributed by Linda DuPuy*

## VEGETABLES WITH RICE

SERVINGS: 4

PREPARATION TIME: 30 mins. for vegetables    COOKING TIME: 10 mins.
45 mins. for rice

1 cup pecan or walnut halves
1 onion, sliced into rings
1 green pepper, cut in strips
1 cup broccoli florets
1 medium zucchini, sliced

1 medium crookneck squash, sliced
1 cup Chinese peas
1-2 tbsp. low sodium soy sauce
2 cups hot cooked brown rice
3 tbsp. chopped fresh parsley or
    coriander

Roast nuts in oven until lightly toasted. Set aside. In a wok or silverstone frying pan, saute the onion, green pepper and broccoli in a small amount of water over high heat for one minute. Add zucchini and squash and stir for another minute. Stir in Chinese peas, add ¼ cup water and the low sodium soy sauce. Cover tightly, cook until vegetables are tender, about 3-5 minutes.

Mix parsley or coriander into the hot rice. Spoon the vegetables over the rice and top with the roasted nuts.

## GREEN BULGUR

### SERVINGS: 6

PREPARATION TIME: 30 mins.    COOKING TIME: none

1 cup bulgur
¾ cup chopped green onions
½ cup chopped fresh coriander
    OR parsley
2 cups frozen peas, thawed under
    cold water
1 tomato, chopped

3 tbsp. lime juice
1 tbsp. low sodium soy sauce
several dashes Tabasco sauce
    (optional)
fresh ground pepper (optional)

Pour 2 cups boiling water over the bulgur. Cover bowl with a towel and let rest for 25 minutes. Meanwhile, prepare green onions, parsley, tomatoes and peas.

After bulgur has soaked for 25 minutes, drain and press out excess water. Combine all ingredients. Mix well. Serve warm or cold.

## AFRICAN MILLET AND BEANS

### SERVINGS: 8-10

PREPARATION TIME: 30 mins.    COOKING TIME: 3 ½ hrs.

1½ cups dried garbanzo beans
10 cups water
1 large onion chopped
1 lb. mushrooms, thickly sliiced
2 potatoes, cut in chunks

2 tsp. ground cumin
1 tsp. turmeric
½ tsp. ground cloves
¹⁄₁₆ tsp. cayenne

1 small head cauliflower,
  cut into large flowerettes
2 tsp. grated gingerroot
2 cloves garlic, crushed

⅓ cup chopped fresh coriander
2 tbsp. lemon juice
2 tbsp. honey
⅓ cup uncooked millet

Cook beans in the water for 2½ hours. Add remaining ingredients except for lemon, honey, coriander and millet. Cook ½ hour longer. Add millet. Cook 30 minutes. Stir in lemon, honey and coriander. Serve with Sweet and Sour Fruit Sauce (recipe in this volume.)

## MEXICAN BULGUR

SERVINGS: 4

PREPARATION TIME: 20 mins.    COOKING TIME: 30 mins.

1 onion, chopped
1 stalk celery, chopped
1 green pepper, chopped
1½ cups bulgur wheat
¼ cup chopped green chilies
  (canned)

2 tsp. chili powder
1 tsp. ground cumin
3 ¼ cups water
2 tbsp. low sodium soy sauce
2 tbsp. finely chopped fresh
  coriander

In a large saucepan, saute the onion, celery and green pepper in ¼ cup water until soft—about 10 minutes. Add bulgur, green chilies and seasonings, except fresh coriander. Cook and stir for a few minutes. Add the remaining water and the soy sauce. Bring to a boil, reduce heat, cover and cook until liquid is absorbed, about 20 minutes. Stir in coriander. Serve as a base for assorted toppings or stuff into pita bread or use to fill a chapati.

HELPFUL HINTS: Some suggested toppings are: chopped tomatoes, chopped green onions, alfalfa sprouts, shredded lettuce, assorted Mexican salsas.

## FRUITED RICE STUFFING

SERVINGS: makes 6 cups

PREPARATION TIME: 30 mins.    COOKING TIME: variable
(cooked rice needed)

5 cups cooked brown rice
1 onion, chopped
½ cup raisins
⅓ cup chopped dried apricots

⅓ cup chopped dried dates
¼ tsp. ground cloves
¼ tsp. allspice

Soak the raisins, apricots, and dates in water to cover for 30 minutes. Drain. Add to cooked rice. Saute the onion in a small amount of water for 5 minutes. Add to rice mixture. Add seasonings and mix well. Use to fill chapati roll-ups or to stuff a favorite vegetable.

HELPFUL HINTS: To make a chapati roll-up dish, place a little stuffing down the center of a chapati, roll up, place seam side down in a baking dish to which 1 cup of a favorite sauce has been spread over the bottom. Repeat with as many chapati as you can fill, then cover with the remainder of the sauce you've chosen. Bake at 350 degrees, covered, about 30 minutes. Some good choices for sauces would be: Heather's Mushroom Delight, Apricot Chutney Sauce, Dill Sauce, Oriental Tomato Sauce, Nutty White Sauce.

To stuff vegetables, follow directions for Stuffed Vegetables, found in this book.

## BAKED MILLET SUPREME

### SERVINGS: 6

PREPARATION TIME: 10 mins.    COOKING TIME: 1¼ hrs.

| | |
|---|---|
| 1 cup millet | 2½ cups water |
| ¼ cup oatmeal | 2 tbsp. low sodium soy sauce |
| 1 cup minced onion | ½ tsp. sage |
| 1 cup minced celery | ½ tsp. ground oregano |
| 1½ cups nut or rice milk | dash or two black pepper (optional) |

Combine millet, oatmeal, onions and celery in a large casserole dish. Mix remaining ingredients together. Pour over mixture in casserole dish—stir gently to mix well. Cover and bake at 350 degrees for 1¼ hours.

## BARLEY VEGETABLE CASSEROLE

### SERVINGS: 8-10

PREPARATION TIME: 30 mins.    COOKING TIME: 1¾ hrs.

| | |
|---|---|
| 2 onions, sliced and separated into rings | 2 zucchini, cut in half and sliced in chunks |
| 2 green peppers, sliced in strips | 1½ cups sliced green beans |
| ½ cup barley | 1 cup frozen peas |
| 1 cup water | 2 cups cauliflower flowerets |
| 2 tbsp. low sodium soy sauce | 2 tomatoes, cut in wedges |
| 1 tsp. pure vegetable seasoning for broth (optional) | 2 tbsp. lemon juice |
| 2 carrots, sliced | 2 cloves garlic, crushed |
| | paprika |
| | pepper |
| | parsley for garnish |

Place onions and green peppers in a large silverstone skillet with about ½ cup water. Cook and stir over high heat until water evaporates. Add another ½ cup water. Continue to cook and stir until onions are soft and golden colored. Remove from heat.

In a large casserole dish, mix barley, water, soy sauce, and pure vegetable seasoning mix. Layer the carrots, zucchini, beans, peas, cauliflower, and tomatoes over the barley mixture. Then top with cooked onions and green peppers. Sprinkle with paprika and black pepper as you add layers.

Combine lemon juice and garlic in a small bowl. Pour over casserole. Cover. Bake at 350 degrees for 1¾ hours. Sprinkle with chopped parsley before serving.

HELPFUL HINTS: See Update on Ingredients (in this volume) for a discussion of the pure vegetable seasonings.

## RICE-TOFU STUFFING MIX

SERVINGS: makes about 5 cups

PREPARATION TIME: 15 mins.     COOKING TIME: 10 mins.
(cooked rice needed)

| | |
|---|---|
| 1 onion, chopped | 1 cup crumbled tofu |
| 2 stalks celery, chopped | 2 tbsp. natural Worcestershire |
| 2 cloves garlic, crushed | sauce |
| ½ lb. mushrooms, sliced | 1 tbsp. low sodium soy sauce |
| ¼ cup water | ½ tsp. paprika |
| 2 cups brown rice, cooked | ½ tsp. dill weed |

Saute the onion, celery, garlic and mushrooms in the water about 8-10 minutes. Stir in remaining ingredients and mix well. Use as a stuffing mix for many different vegetables or use to fill chapaties or corn tortillas.

HELPFUL HINTS: This mixture needs to be baked inside it's chosen casing for about 30 minutes, either with or without sauce to cover it. Some suggestions for use are: stuffed green peppers, stuffed acorn squash, stuffed chapati roll-ups. See recipes for Stuffed Vegetables or Stuffed Chapati Rolls in this volume.

# Main Dishes
## General

### VEGETABLE MANAPUA

SERVINGS: makes 24

PREPARATION TIME: at least 2 hrs.     COOKING TIME: 15-20 mins.
(in shifts)

FILLING:

½ lb. mushrooms, finely chopped
1 onion, finely chopped
2 cloves garlic, pressed
2 tsp. grated ginger root
1 cup chopped water chestnuts
1 cup chopped bamboo shoots
½ cup thinly sliced green onions

4 tbsp. low sodium soy sauce
2 tbsp. sherry (or apple juice)
1 tsp. honey
⅓ cup water
1 tbsp. cornstarch or arrowroot
2 tbsp. chopped fresh coriander
(optional)

DOUGH:

2 cups warm water (110 degrees)
2 pkg. active dry yeast
1 tbsp. honey

5 cups whole wheat flour
(a little more or less—depending
on how much you use for
kneading)

DOUGH: Prepare the dough first. While it is rising, prepare the filling mixture.

In a large bowl, dissolve yeast in water, add honey. Mix well. Set aside until bubbly (about 15 minutes). Gradually add the flour, mixing with a spoon, until dough holds together. Turn dough onto a floured bread board. Knead until smooth and elastic, adding enough flour so dough is not sticky (about 10 min.). Place dough in a clean bowl. Cover with a damp towel and set in a warm place. Allow to rise until doubled in bulk (about 1 hour).

Now prepare the filling mixture as directed below.

Turn dough onto lightly floured board. Knead briefly. Divide into 24 equal pieces. Roll each piece into a 5 inch circle with rolling pin. Use some flour as you roll to prevent sticking. Make the outside edges slightly thinner for easier assembly.

FILLING: Combine soy sauce, sherry, honey, water and cornstarch. Mix well. Add some chopped fresh coriander, if desired. Set aside. Place the mushrooms, onions, garlic and ginger in a large pan with ¼ cup water. Cook and stir over high heat for 3 minutes. Add water chestnuts, bamboo shoots and green onions. Cook and stir an additional 3 minutes. Stir in the sauce mixture. Continue to cook and stir until sauce bubbles and thickens. Remove from heat. Set aside to cool.

TO ASSEMBLE: Place a heaping tablespoon of filling mixture in the center of the circle. Bring edges of dough up to the center and pinch together to seal the filling inside. Place each manapua, folded side down on a 2 inch square of ti leaf, parchment paper or aluminum foil. Repeat until all are filled. Place on a baking sheet, cover and let rise in a warm place for 30 minutes.

Then place a few in a steamer (one layer only) over boiling water. Cover and steam for 20 minutes. Serve warm.

HELPFUL HINTS: This takes a lot of time and effort to prepare, but the results are worth it. It makes the job easier if you have someone to help you. My daughter, Heather, usually helps me make these because she also loves to eat them. They are excellent to take on a picnic or in a lunch bag. I usually make them ahead of time, keep them in the refrigerator, then steam for 5-10 minutes to serve warm. They may also be eaten cold.

These manapua can be filled with many different fillings. Usually ones that do not have too much sauce work best. These may also be baked in a 350 degree oven for 15-20 minutes.

## VEGETABLE PIE

SERVINGS: 8

PREPARATION TIME: 45 mins.    COOKING TIME: 45 mins.

1 recipe nutty pie crust (found in this volume)

FILLING:

| | |
|---|---|
| 1 onion, sliced | 1 tbsp. natural Worcestershire sauce |
| ½ lb. mushrooms, sliced | ½ tsp. basil |
| 2 cups sliced broccoli | ½ tsp. dry mustard |
| 2 cups sliced cauliflower | ½ tsp. dill weed |
| 2 cups sliced carrots | ½ tsp. cumin |
| 1 clove garlic, pressed | Several dashes white pepper (optional) |
| 2 cups water | 2 tbsp. bran (optional) to sprinkle on the top |
| 2 tbsp. cornstarch or arrowroot | |
| 3 tbsp. low sodium soy sauce | |

Prepare pie crust according to directions found in this book. Prebake for 10 minutes at 350 degrees. Set aside.

Prepare filling mixture by sauteing onion, mushrooms and garlic in ½ cup water for 5 minutes. Add the remaining sliced vegetables. Cook and stir over medium-high heat an additional 5 minutes. Combine remaining ingredients (except bran). Add to vegetables. Cook and stir until thickened and bubbly. Pour into piecrust. Sprinkle with bran, if desired. Bake in a 350 degree oven for 45 minutes. Cool for 15 minutes before cutting.

## TEMPEH AND GRAIN CASSEROLE

### SERVINGS: 6-8

PREPARATION TIME: 10 mins.    COOKING TIME: 1¾ hrs.

1 onion, chopped
½ cup wheat berries
1 tbsp. curry powder
4 cups water

1 cup raw brown rice
4 cups frozen mixed vegetables
2 cups cubed tempeh
2 tbsp. low sodium soy sauce

In a large pot, saute the onion in ½ cup water for 3 minutes. Stir in wheat berries and curry powder. Add remaining water. Bring to a boil, cover, reduce heat and cook for 30 minutes. Add the rice. Cook an additional 30 minutes. Add vegetables, tempeh and soy sauce. Mix well, turn into a casserole dish. Bake, covered, at 350 degrees for 35 minutes.

HELPFUL HINTS: May be prepared ahead up until baking time. If refrigerated, add an additional 10 minutes to baking time. See Update on Ingredients for a discussion on tempeh.

*Contributed by Brandon Stone*

## POTATOES WITH DILL

### SERVINGS: 4

PREPARATION TIME: 30 mins.    COOKING TIME: 20 mins.
(cooked potatoes needed)

6 cups chunked, cooked potatoes
½ lb. mushrooms, sliced
2-4 cloves garlic, pressed
1 bunch fresh dill, chopped or 1
    tablespoon dried dill weed

¼ tsp. black pepper
2 tbsp. vinegar
¼ cup water

Saute mushrooms, dill and garlic in the water about 10 minutes. Add potatoes, pepper and vinegar. Cook until potatoes are heated through. Add a little water if necessary to prevent sticking.

# LASAGNA ROLL-UPS

### SERVINGS: 8-10

PREPARATION TIME: 1½ hrs.    COOKING TIME: 45 mins.

20 spinach lasagna noodles
1 cup chopped onions
2 lbs. fresh spinach, chopped
2 cups mashed tofu
¼ cup whole wheat flour
1 tbsp. low sodium soy sauce

2 tsp. oregano
½ tsp. dillweed
1 tsp. basil
8 cups Marinara Sauce (recipe in The McDougall Plan)

Cook lasagna noodles in boiling water until tender—about 8 minutes. Drain and set aside in cold water.

Wash spinach, remove tough stems and chop. Set aside. Using a large pan, saute the onion in ½ cup water until soft—about 5 minutes. Add the chopped spinach and saute until limp. Add tofu, soy sauce, oregano, basil and dillweed. Mix well. Stir in ¼ cup whole wheat flour. Mix. Set aside.

Remove lasagna noodles from water and hang over sink edges to drain. Take the noodles, one at a time, and lay flat. Spread about 2 tablespoons tofu mixture along the entire length of noodles, then roll-up the noodle. Repeat until all noodles are filled and rolled.

Place about 2 cups of the Marinara sauce in the bottom of a large oblong baking dish (13x15).

Place roll-ups seam side down in baking dish. Pour remaining sauce over the rolls. Cover. Bake at 350 degrees for 45 minutes.

HELPFUL HINTS: This makes a wonderful meal for entertaining. It does take some extra time to prepare, but the result is worth it. A 10 oz. package of frozen chopped spinach may be substituted for the fresh spinach, if desired. Thaw the spinach in a colander, press out the excess water, and add directly to the tofu mixture without steaming.

This mixture may also be used to fill manicotti. Fill with stuffing mixture, cover with Marinara Sauce (found in The McDougall Plan), and bake as directed above. This mixture will fill 14 manicotti.

# SPRING ROLLS

SERVINGS: 20-30 rolls

PREPARATION TIME: 90 mins.    COOKING TIME: 25 mins.

7 cups finely chopped or shredded vegetables (use broccoli, cauliflower, Chinese cabbage, celery, etc.)
1 cup finely chopped green onions
½ cup water
1 pkg. dried Shiitake mushrooms (0.7 oz.)
2 cups mung bean sprouts

½ cup crumbled previously frozen tofu (optional)
½ tbsp. grated fresh gingerroot
1 clove garlic, crushed
2 tbsp. low sodium soy sauce
1 tbsp. sherry (optional)
1½ tbsp. cornstarch or arrowroot mixed in ½ cup water
2-3 tbsp. chopped fresh coriander (optional)

Soak the dried mushrooms in 1½ cups hot water for 30 minutes. Squeeze out excess water. Slice in thin strips. Meanwhile, place the 7 cups assorted vegetables, the green onions and the water in a large pot. Cook over medium-high heat for 10 minutes, stirring often. Add mushroom strips, mung bean sprouts and optional tofu, if desired. Cook and stir another 10 minutes. Add seasonings (except for thickener). Cook another 10 minutes. Add thickening mixture, cook and stir until thickened. Stir in fresh coriander, if desired.

Place about ⅛ cup of filling in the center of a spring roll wrapper. Fold up bottom, fold over sides; then fold down top. Place on a non-stick or very lightly oiled baking sheet. Repeat until all filling is used. Bake at 400 degrees for 15 minutes, then reduce heat to 350 degrees, turn over with spatula and bake 10 minutes longer. Serve with a Sweet and Sour sauce or Oriental dipping sauce (recipes in this volume.)

HELPFUL HINTS: These may be prepared ahead until the baking time. Cover with plastic wrap and place in refrigerator until ready to bake.

Depending on which area of the country you live in, you may or may not have good luck in finding acceptable spring roll wrappers. They are sometimes called Egg Roll wrappers or lumpia wrappers. Some natural food stores may stock these wrappers, or you may have to look in an Oriental market. This mixture could also be used to fill chapatis if you are unable to find healthy pastry wrappers. These are also good cold as an appetizer or packed in a lunch box.

*Contributed by Don and Carol Brown*

## CHINESE VEGETABLES

SERVINGS: 4

PREPARATION TIME: 30 mins.    COOKING TIME: 10-15 mins.

**VEGETABLES:**

1 small bunch broccoli, cut into
  bite-sized pieces
4 green onions, chopped
2 cloves garlic, minced
4 slices fresh gingerroot, minced
½ lb. mushrooms, sliced

20 snow peas
1 cup bean sprouts
1 can baby corn, drained
1 can bamboo shoots, sliced and
  drained
1 can water chestnuts, sliced and
  drained

**SEASONING SAUCE:**

4 tbsp. low sodium soy sauce
6 tbsp. water
2 tbsp. cornstarch

2 tsp. honey
2 tbsp. white wine

Combine seasoning ingredients and set aside. Blanch the broccoli in a pan of water and 2 tablespoons of vinegar for 1 minute. Cool under running water (this will soften and maintain the dark green color of the broccoli).

Saute onions, garlic and ginger in a small amount of water in a wok or a large pan for a few minutes. Add mushrooms, cook for 2 minutes. Add remaining vegetables and the broccoli. Stir and cook for 1 minute. Cover and steam for 1 minute. Add seasoning sauce. Cook and stir until thickened. Serve over brown rice.

*Contributed by Dr. and Mrs. W. Shrader*

## SEVEN LAYER CASSEROLE

SERVINGS: 6-8

PREPARATION TIME: 20 mins.    COOKING TIME: 1½ hrs.
(cooked beans needed)

1 cup uncooked brown rice
1 cup cooked kidney beans
1 cup potatoes, diced
1 cup frozen green peas
1 cup green pepper, diced

1 cup frozen corn
1 cup onions, diced
2 (8 oz.) cans tomato sauce
¾ cup water
freshly ground black pepper

Using a large casserole dish, layer the rice, beans, potatoes and peas. Sprinkle with some pepper, if desired. Pour 1 (8 oz.) can of tomato sauce over the layers, then pour ½ cup water in. Continue layering the green pepper, corn and onions. Sprinkle with a little more black pepper. Pour in the second can of tomato sauce and the remaining ¼ cup of water.

Cover and bake at 350 degrees for 1 hour, then uncover and continue to cook for 30 minutes longer.

HELPFUL HINTS: May be prepared ahead up to baking time. May also be used to stuff vegetables. Follow general directions for stuffed vegetables in this book.

# DILLY STUFFED CABBAGE

SERVINGS: 6-8

PREPARATION TIME: 45 mins.    COOKING TIME: 45 mins.
(cooked rice needed)

STUFFED CABBAGE:

| | |
|---|---|
| 1 large head cabbage | 1 tsp. dill weed |
| 1 onion, chopped | 1 tsp. oregano |
| ½ lb. mushrooms, chopped | ½ tsp. curry powder |
| 1 carrot, grated | 1 tbsp. parsley flakes |
| 1 bunch green onions, chopped | ¼ tsp. black pepper |
| 2 tbsp. low sodium soy sauce | 3 cups cooked brown rice |

SAUCE:

| | |
|---|---|
| 4 cups tomato sauce | 1 tsp. oregano |
| 1 tbsp. dill weed | several dashes Tabasco |
| 1 tsp. basil | |

Remove core from cabbage. Steam over boiling water for 5 minutes. Let cool slightly. Peel leaves off carefully and set aside. (After you peel off some of the outer layers you may need to steam the cabbage again to soften the inner leaves.)

Saute onions, mushrooms, carrots and green onions in ½ cup water for 10 minutes. Stir in soy sauce, dill, oregano, curry powder, parsley flakes, and black pepper. Cook and stir for a few minutes. Add rice. Mix well and set aside.

Combine sauce ingredients in a bowl. Stir 1 cup of sauce into the rice mixture. Pour 1 cup of the sauce over the bottom of a 9"X12" non-stick baking dish.

Spoon about ⅓ to ½ cup of rice mixture into the center of each cabbage leaf. Roll up and place in the baking dish. Pour remaining sauce over the rolls in the baking dish. Cover. Bake at 350 degrees for 45 minutes.

HELPFUL HINTS: May be prepared ahead. Refrigerate. Bake just before serving and add 15 minutes to baking time.

## POTATO-VEGGIE DINNER

SERVINGS: variable

PREPARATION TIME: 30 mins.     COOKING TIME: 1-1½ hrs.

baked white potatoes
Assorted chopped steamed veggies

Sauce of your choice: Marinara,
  Mushroom Gravy,
  Chickenless A'La King, Chili, etc.
  (found in the McDougall Books)

For each serving, slice a large baked potato in half on a plate. Cover potato with some steamed vegetables (1 to 2 cups, your choice of varieties). Then cover it all with about 1 cup of a favorite sauce of your choice.

HELPFUL HINTS: This can be made quickly if you have a microwave oven. Bake the potatoes in the microwave, then heat up a bag of assorted chopped packaged-frozen vegetables, make a quick gravy or use a sauce you have left over from another meal.

## TOFU LOAF

SERVINGS: makes one loaf for 3-6 people

PREPARATION TIME: 20 mins.     COOKING TIME: 1 hr.
                               RESTING TIME: 15 mins.

2 lbs. tofu, crumbled
1½ cups whole wheat bread
  crumbs
½ cup chopped parsley
½ lb. mushrooms, chopped
½ cup celery, chopped
1 onion, chopped
1 clove garlic, pressed

3 tbsp. low sodium soy sauce
1 tbsp. Worcestershire sauce
1 tbsp. Dijon mustard
¼ tsp black pepper
¼ cup vegetable broth, water, nut
  milk or rice milk

Combine the tofu with the bread crumbs and parsley, and set aside. Saute the mushrooms, celery, onions and garlic in about ¼ cup water for 5 minutes. Add tofu mixture. Add remaining ingredients and mix well. Turn into a non-stick pan and press down with hand. Bake at 350 degrees for 1 hour. Remove from heat and let rest for 15 minutes before slicing. (Loosen sides with a spatula and invert over a serving platter to remove from pan.)

HELPFUL HINTS: This can be prepared ahead and refrigerated until baking time. Leftovers make wonderful sandwich fillers. If you do not have a non-stick pan, you will need to lightly oil your loaf pan before pressing the tofu mixture into it.

*Contributed by Carol Emerick*
## POTATO KIBBY

SERVINGS: 6

PREPARATION TIME: 45 mins.    COOKING TIME: 45 mins

KIBBY:

2 lbs potatoes                          1 cup whole wheat flour
1 cup cracked wheat

FILLING:

1 onion, sliced                         1 tsp. lemon juice
1 cup pine nuts

KIBBY: Boil potatoes until tender. Peel and mash. Soak cracked wheat in 2 cups hot water until soft. Knead mashed potatoes and softened wheat together thoroughly. Blend in flour. Form into football-shaped kibbies, each about the size of a small lime. Perforate one end with thumb and fill with 1 tsp. filling in each kibby. Place kibbies in a silverstone pan and cook over medium heat until golden brown.

FILLING: Saute onions in a small amount of water for 10 minutes. Add pine nuts and cook with onions, stirring frequently. Remove from heat. Stir in lemon juice. Use 1 tsp. to stuff each kibby.

## BAKED TOFU CUBES

SERVINGS: variable

PREPARATION TIME: 5 mins.    COOKING TIME: 15 mins.

1 lb. firm tofu, drained

Pat tofu with a towel until it is dry. Press under a bread board with a ½ lb. weight on top for ½ hour to squeeze some of the excess water out of the tofu. Carefully cut into 1 inch pieces. Place a very light coating of oil on a wire cake rack (use a paper towel to do this). Place cake rack on baking sheet and then arrange tofu pieces on the rack (leave a little space between each one.) Bake at 300 degrees for 15 minutes, until they are starting to brown. Remove from oven.

Use in recipes as a meat or seafood substitute.

## *Contributed by Don and Carol Brown*
## THERMOS PLATE LUNCH

SERVINGS: variable

PREPARATION TIME: variable    COOKING TIME: none

Choose leftover vegetables or grains. Reheat a portion of each in the microwave or on top of the stove and put the heated foods into separate ziplock bags. Then put the bags into a wide mouth thermos that has been preheated with hot water. You can carry 3-4 separate dishes this way. With a piece of bread or fruit you have an interesting plate lunch.

## ITALIAN DRESSED SPAGHETTI

SERVINGS: 4

PREPARATION TIME: 30 mins. COOKING TIME: 20 mins.

2 cups broccoli pieces
2 cups cauliflower flowerettes
2 cups zucchini pieces (1 inch)
½ cup oil free Italian Dressing
2 cups tomato, chopped
½ lb. mushroom halves

¼ cup chopped parsley
½ tbsp. cornstarch or arrowroot
½ cup oil free Italian Dressing
½ cup nut or rice milk
½ lb. spinach spaghetti, cooked
    and drained

Cook cauliflower, broccoli and zucchini in ½ cup water and ½ cup dressing for 5 minutes. Add tomatoes, mushrooms and parsley. Cook an additional 10 minutes. Mix 1 tbsp. cornstarch in a small amount of water. Add to vegetable mixture while stirring. Cook and stir for 1 minute. Remove from heat and place in serving bowl.

Mix ½ cup dressing with acceptable milk. Heat just to boiling. Pour over hot cooked spaghetti and toss to mix well. Place in serving bowl. Serve the noodles as a base for the vegetable mixture.

# ORIENTAL DRESSED NOODLES

SERVINGS: 6

PREPARATION TIME: 40 mins. COOKING TIME: 20 mins.

½ cup water
½ tsp. mustard powder
2 cloves garlic, crushed
1 tbsp. grated gingerroot
1 bunch green onions, cut in 1
  inch pieces
1 carrot, thinly sliced
1 cup cauliflower pieces
1 cup broccoli pieces
¼ lb. Chinese peas
1 cup Chinese cabbage, sliced

½ lb. mushrooms, cut in half
¼ cup fresh chopped coriander
  leaves
1 cup water
2 tbsp. sherry
2 tbsp. low sodium soy sauce
⅛ tsp. Chinese 5-Spice
several dashes Cayenne pepper
2 tbsp. cornstarch or arrowroot
8 oz. hot cooked soba or udon
  noodles

Place ½ cup water in wok or large pan. Add garlic, ginger and mustard. Add green onion, carrot, cauliflower and broccoli. Saute for 5 minutes. Add remaining vegetables and another ½ cup of water. Cover and simmer for 10 minutes. Combine the remaining ½ cup water, sherry, soy sauce, 5-spice, pepper and cornstarch. Mix well. Add to vegetables. Cook and stir until thickened. Mix with the cooked noodles. Serve at once.

*Contributed by Joan Brandwen*

# SPINACH-TOFU BURGERS

SERVINGS: 6-8

PREPARATION TIME: 30 mins.    COOKING TIME: 15 mins.

1 lb. tofu, cut into cubes
1 onion, chopped
1 pkg. (10 oz.) chopped spinach
  (frozen)
½ cup chopped cashews
2 tbsp. low sodium soy sauce

¼ tsp. nutmeg
½ tsp. basil
1 tbsp. egg replacer well mixed
  with 3 tbsp. water.

Saute onions in a small amount of water until tender. Set aside. Thaw spinach, then cook over low heat for 2-3 minutes (or microwave, high, ½ minute). Set aside.

Combine spinach, onion, tofu and the seasonings in a food processor, and chop. Add egg replacer and water (mixed until frothy). Add nuts. Process with off/on motion until blended. Shape into patties. Cook on a non-stick griddle until lightly browned.

Serve on whole wheat buns with sprouts, sliced onions, tomatoes, and condiments.

*Contributed by Lila Pang*

## KOREAN RICE AND POTATOES

SERVINGS: 4

PREPARATION TIME: 15 mins.    COOKING TIME: 45 mins.

4 cups water
2 cups brown rice

1 cup small cubes of white or
   sweet potatoes

Wash and rinse the rice. Place in a sauce pan with a tight fitting lid. Add the potatoes and then the cold water. Cover and bring to a quick rolling boil. Turn heat down to low and cook for 30-40 minutes or until tender.

HELPFUL HINTS: A ½ cup of green peas may be added, if desired, for color and flavor.

## STUFFED VEGETABLES

SERVINGS: variable

PREPARATION TIME: 15-30 mins.    COOKING TIME: variable

All vegetables need some liquid in the baking dish. See helpful hints.

SQUASH:

1-2 acorn squash cut in half, seeds
   scraped out.

Place in baking dish with ½ inch water on bottom. Bake for 1 hour at 350 degrees. Stuff with a favorite filling. Cover. Return to oven and bake an additional 30 minutes.

GREEN PEPPERS:

4-6 green peppers cut in half,
   seeds cleaned out.

Steam over boiling water for 5 minutes. Fill with a favorite stuffing. Cover. Bake in a 350 degree oven for 30 minutes.

**EGGPLANTS:**

1-2 eggplants.

Cut in half, insides scooped out leaving ¼ inch along the sides. (Save the insides for another recipe, or dice them and add to the stuffing mixture.) Fill with stuffing, cover and bake at 350 degrees for 30-40 minutes.

**ZUCCHINI:**

4-6 zucchini.

Cut off tops, scoop out insides, leaving ¼ inch along the sides. (Reserve insides for another time, or dice and add to stuffing mixture.) Steam over boiling water for 5 minutes. Fill with stuffing mixture. Cover. Bake at 350 degrees for 30 minutes.

**ONIONS:**

4-6 onions.

Cook the onions in a small amount of water for 15 minutes. Drain. Cut a slice off the stem end and scoop out some of the center, leaving several layers on the outside. Fill with stuffing mixture. Place in baking dish, cover and bake at 350 degrees for 45 minutes.

**TOMATOES:**

6 tomatoes.

Cut off tops of tomatoes, scoop out insides. (Reserve for another use, or add to stuffing mixture.) Fill with stuffing mixture. Place in baking dish, cover and bake at 350 degrees for 20 minutes.

HELPFUL HINTS: While baking stuffed vegetables, it is necessary to have some liquid in the bottom of the baking dish to prevent the vegetables from getting dried out. Use water or vegetable stock, tomato juice, or another liquid, usually about ½ inch in the bottom of the baking dish. Cover with aluminum foil and bake as directed.

## WHERE'S THE MEAT LOAF?

SERVINGS: makes 1 loaf

PREPARATION TIME: 30 mins.     COOKING TIME: 1 hr.
                                RESTING TIME: 15 mins.

| | |
|---|---|
| 2 lbs. tofu, mashed | 2 tbsp. Dijon mustard |
| 1⅔ cups rolled oats | 2 tbsp. Worcestershire sauce |
| ⅓ cup tomato sauce (or acceptable Ketchup) | 2 tbsp. barbeque sauce (or more tomato sauce) |
| ¼ cup low sodium soy sauce | ¼ tsp. garlic powder |
| 1 onion, finely chopped | ¼ tsp. black pepper (optional) |

Combine all ingredients in a large bowl. Mix well. Press mixture into a non-stick loaf pan. Bake at 350 degrees for 1 hour. Remove from oven. Let rest for 15 minutes, then loosen sides gently with a spatula and invert over a serving platter to remove.

HELPFUL HINTS: Leftovers make excellent sandwich fillings. If you do not have a non-stick loaf pan, you will need to lightly oil the bottom of your loaf pan before pressing in the tofu mixture. Do not use quick cooking oats in this recipe, they do not absorb enough liquid and the loaf stays too moist.

## PASTA PRIMAVERA

### SERVINGS: 4

PREPARATION TIME: 30 mins.    COOKING TIME: 15 mins.

| | |
|---|---|
| ½ lb. whole wheat or vegetable spaghetti | 1 tsp. basil |
| 3 cloves garlic, crushed | ½ tsp. oregano |
| 1 small onion, sliced | ¼ cup chopped parsley |
| 6-8 mushrooms, sliced | 2 tbsp. low sodium soy sauce |
| 1 zucchini, julienned | 3 tbsp. tomato paste |
| 1 green pepper, julienned | 1 cup water |
| 1 cup chopped broccoli | 1 tomato, chopped |

Cook pasta in boiling water until tender, about 10 minutes.

While pasta is cooking, saute the vegetables and garlic in ½ cup water for 5 minutes. Add the seasonings, tomato paste and water. Cook and stir over medium-high heat until vegetables are crisp-tender, about 5 minutes. Add chopped tomato and cook for a few minutes to soften slightly.

Add vegetables to pasta and toss lightly. Serve at once.

*Contributed by Dr. and Mrs. W. Shrader*

## OAT BURGERS

### SERVINGS: 10-11 patties

PREPARATION TIME: 20 mins.    COOKING TIME: 30 mins.

| | |
|---|---|
| 1 lb. block firm tofu | 1 tbsp. tahini |
| 1½ cups oatmeal, uncooked | 2 tbsp. natural Worcestershire |
| 1 onion, chopped | sauce |
| ½ cup grated carrots | 1 tbsp. low sodium soy sauce |

Saute onion in a small amount of water until translucent. Drain the tofu and crumble it into a large bowl.

Combine all the ingredients and mix together well. (Use your hands, if necessary). Shape into patties, moistening hands with water occasionally to prevent sticking. Place patties on a non-stick baking sheet. Bake at 350 degrees for 20 minutes. Turn over once and bake for an additional 10 minutes. Serve as is, or place briefly under broiler to brown them.

HELPFUL HINTS: These may be prepared ahead and placed under the broiler for a few minutes before serving. They can also be heated quickly in a microwave. They are also very good cold. Great to bring to a picnic or cook-out.

Sometimes you may get tofu with a high water content. As a result, you may find the ingredients difficult to form into patties using your hands. If this should happen, you can add a few more oats, then form into small rounds, place on non-stick baking sheet and press into desired shape using your finger tips.

## JAPANESE UDON AND VEGETABLES

### SERVINGS: 6-8

**PREPARATION TIME:** 45 mins.    **COOKING TIME:** 30 mins.

| | |
|---|---|
| ½ cup water | 30 snow peas, cleaned and |
| 3 tbsp. low sodium soy sauce | left whole |
| 1 tsp. grated fresh gingerroot | 4 cups (packed) shredded cabbage |
| ⅛ tsp. powdered horseradish | (Chinese cabbage or head |
| 1 large onion, cut in half, | cabbage) |
| then thinly sliced | ¼ cup Kombu stock (or water) |
| 1 bunch green onions, cut in | ⅓ cup Umeboshi plum sauce |
| pieces | (see Update on Ingredients) |
| 2 carrots, thinly sliced | 8 oz. Udon, boiled in 2 qts. water |
| 1 cup thinly sliced cauliflower | until tender |
| flowerettes | |

In a large pan or wok, place the water, soy sauce, gingerroot and horseradish and bring to a boil. Add onion, green onions, carrots, cauliflower and snow peas. Saute for a few minutes until all are well coated. Add cabbage and Kombu stock. Saute a few more minutes. Add plum sauce, mix in well. Cover, simmer for 10 minutes over medium heat.

In the meantime, cook the udon until tender about 7-8 minutes. Drain, rinse under cool water. Add to cooked vegetables. Mix well. Thicken mixture with about 1 tbsp. cornstarch or arrowroot mixed in ¼ cup water. Add to vegetable-noodle mixture, cook and stir until thickened.

May be served hot or cold.

# VEGETABLE BURRITOS

### SERVINGS: 8-10

### PREPARATION TIME: 45 mins.    COOKING TIME: 30 mins.

SAUCE:

1 onion, chopped
2 cloves garlic, pressed
⅓ cup canned green chilies, chopped
1 tbsp. chili powder
1 tsp. ground cumin

½ tsp. ground coriander
⅛ tsp. cayenne
1 (8 oz.) can tomato sauce
1 (6 oz.) can tomato paste
3 ½ cups water

FILLING:

1 onion, chopped
1 green pepper, chopped
½ lb. mushrooms, chopped
1 cup corn kernels
3 cups chopped zucchini

1½ tsp. chili powder
1 tsp. ground cumin
12-15 chapatis—whole wheat flour tortillas

SAUCE: Saute onion and garlic in ½ cup water for 5 minutes. Add green chilies and spices. Stir and saute a few minutes. Add remaining ingredients. Mix well and simmer for 15 minutes. Set aside.

FILLING: Saute onion, green pepper and mushrooms in ½ cup water for 5 minutes. Add corn, zucchini and spices. Saute about 10 more minutes. Set aside.

TO ASSEMBLE: Place about ⅓ to ½ cup filling down the center of a chapati. Roll up. Place seam side down in a baking dish to which 1 cup of sauce has been spread over the bottom. Fill, roll and place the remaining burritos in the baking dish. Pour the rest of the sauce over the burritos. Cover. Bake at 350 degrees for 30 minutes.

# STUFFED CHAPATI ROLLS

SERVINGS: variable

PREPARATION TIME: variable    COOKING TIME: 30 mins.

12-18 chapatis
3-5 cups filling mixture
3-5 cups sauce

In a large baking dish, place about 1 cup of sauce over the bottom to prevent the chapati rolls from sticking. Place a small amount of the filling mixture down the center of each chapati. Roll up and place seam side down in the baking dish. Repeat until all chapati are filled. Pour the sauce over the filled chapati. Cover. Bake at 350 degrees for 30 minutes.

HELPFUL HINTS: Some suggestions for fillings and sauces follow.

FILLINGS:

Fruited Rice Stuffing
Spring Roll Filling
Chinese Spicy Vegetables
Rice Tofu Stuffing Mix

TVP Stuffing Mix
Spicy Lentil Filling
Quick Confetti Rice

SAUCES:

Almond Sauce
Apricot Chutney Sauce
Dill Sauce
Heather's Mushroom Delight

Oriental Tomato Sauce
Nutty White Sauce
Marinara Sauce
Curry Sauce

# BAMBOO STEAMED FRESH VEGETABLES

SERVINGS: 2

PREPARATION TIME: 20-30 mins.    COOKING TIME: 10-15 mins.

whole baby carrots
cauliflower florets
broccoli florets
whole mushrooms

patty pan squash, halved
whole Brussels sprouts
small red potatoes, halved
green beans, halved

Prepare an assortment of fresh vegetables; enough to fill a bamboo steamer basket. Use those suggested above or choose some of your favorites. Arrange vegetables in groups around the steamer basket, alternating colors and shapes for visual appeal. Cover basket, steam over boiling water for 10 to 15 minutes, until vegetables are crisp-tender. Serve in steamer basket with sauces to dip vegetables into.

HELPFUL HINTS: This is a very attractive way to serve steamed vegetables. If you do not have a bamboo steamer, you may also do this in a stainless steel steamer basket that fits into a pot. Steam all the vegetables, then arrange them in groups on a platter before serving.

The Hyatt Hotel's "casual dining" restaurants serve a meal similar to this in a bamboo basket.

Choose one of the many sauces in the McDougall books, such as Oriental Dipping Sauce, or any of the many tofu-based sauces. Or try one of these simple sauces:

GINGER-SOY SAUCE:

¼ cup low sodium soy sauce      2 tsp. minced gingerroot
2 tbsp. water      2 tsp. minced green onions
2 tbsp. lemon juice

ONION-HORSERADISH SAUCE:

½ cup soft-blended tofu      2 tsp. minced green onions
1 tsp. pure prepared horseradish      2 tsp. minced parsley

# LEAFY GREEN CHAPATIS

### SERVINGS: Fills 17-18 chapatis

### PREPARATION TIME: 90 mins.    COOKING TIME: 60 mins.

2 onions, chopped      2 cloves garlic, pressed
1 cup celery, thinly sliced      2 tbsp. low sodium soy sauce
2 carrots, grated      1 tsp. ground cumin
2 cups chopped broccoli      1 tsp. ground coriander
2 cups chopped cauliflower      1 tsp. turmeric
6 cups shredded greens (kale,      dash or two of cayenne
  collards, romaine, etc.)      1 tsp. garam masala (recipe in
1 cup shredded green cabbage        Volume I) OR curry powder
1 green pepper, thinly sliced      17-18 Chapatis

SAUCE: 4 cups of sauce are needed. Your choice of sauce to pour over the filled and rolled chapatis. Apricot Chutney Sauce is delicious. For a different flavor, try Curry Sauce, Ginger White Sauce, Oriental Spice Gravy, Creamy Mushroom Sauce or choose one of your favorites.

CHAPATIS: Place all the vegetables in a large pot with about ½ to ¾ cup water. Cook over medium-high heat about 15 minutes, stirring frequently. Add seasonings. Cook an additional 5 minutes. Remove from heat.

Pour about 1 cup sauce in the bottom of a non-stick baking dish. Place about ½ cup vegetable filling down the center of the chapati. Roll up. Place seam side down in baking dish.
Pour Apricot Chutney Sauce (or sauce of your choice) over the top. Cover. Bake at 350 degrees for 30 minutes.

HELPFUL HINTS: If you have a food processor, the chopping time for the vegetables is greatly reduced! This is a delicious use for leafy green vegetables.

*Contributed by Alan Titchenal*
## THAI BASIL PASTA

SERVINGS: 4

PREPARATION TIME: 20 mins.     COOKING TIME: 20 mins.

2 cloves garlic, pressed
½ cup onions, chopped
1 pkg. tempeh, cut in cubes
  (optional)
1 tbsp. low sodium soy sauce
¼ tsp. black pepper

½ tsp. Louisiana hot sauce
1 cup tomato sauce
1 cup leaves of fresh Thai basil, chopped
8 oz. whole wheat udon or other pasta

Boil some water and start cooking the pasta. Saute the garlic and onions in ¼ cup of water for 5 minutes. Add tempeh, soy sauce, and pepper, and saute for 5 minutes. Add hot sauce and tomato sauce and continue to cook 10 minutes more. Remove from heat. Stir in Thai basil and cooked pasta.

HELPFUL HINTS: If you can't find Thai basil you can use regular fresh basil. Or you can use 3 to 4 cups of other chopped leafy greens (spinach, kale, mustard), plus 1 tablespoon of toasted sesame seeds. Even frozen spinach will work. Instead of the tempeh, you can use chunks of tofu or cooked gluten.

# BEANOODLE CASSEROLE

SERVINGS: 8-10

PREPARATION TIME: 45 mins.    COOKING TIME: 60 mins.

1 onion, chopped
2 stalks celery, chopped
2 carrots, grated
1 large potato, grated
1 cup frozen corn
3 ½ cups water
½ cup whole wheat flour
2 tbsp. low sodium soy sauce
2 cups nut milk or rice milk
2 tbsp. parsley flakes

2 tsp. basil
½ tsp. sage
¼ tsp. mustard powder
¼ tsp. dill weed
¼ tsp. white pepper
2 tomatoes, sliced
2 cups cooked kidney beans
8 oz. uncooked macaroni
(whole wheat or vegetable)

Saute onion and celery in ½ cup water for 5 minutes. Add ½ cup whole wheat flour and stir for a few minutes.

Slowly add the remaining water while stirring. Add carrots, potatoes, corn, seasonings and acceptable milk. Cook over medium heat, stirring occasionally, until it thickens. Remove from heat.

Put 1 cup of this sauce in the bottom of a large casserole dish.
Then layer in half of the noodles, half of the kidney beans and half of the remaining sauce. Repeat with noodles, beans and the rest of the sauce.

Slice the tomatoes and lay them over the top. Sprinkle with some chopped fresh coriander or chopped fresh parsley. Cover and bake at 350 degrees for 60 minutes.

# ITALIAN POTATO CASSEROLE

SERVINGS: 4-6

PREPARATION TIME: 15-20 mins.    COOKING TIME: 1¼ hrs.

4 large salad potatoes
1 onion, sliced
3 ½ cups cut fresh green beans

1 can (28 oz.) ground tomatoes
2 cloves garlic, pressed
2 tsp. Italian herb seasoning

Scrub the potatoes, chop into large chunks. Mix the ground tomatoes with the garlic and Italian seasoning. Place all the vegetables in a large casserole dish. Pour the tomato mixture over the vegetables. Add some fresh ground pepper, if desired. Cover and bake at 375 degrees for 1¼ hours. Stir occasionally, if desired.

# PEA AND POTATO CURRY

### SERVINGS: 6

PREPARATION TIME: 30 mins.    COOKING TIME: 20 mins.
(cooked potatoes needed)

2 onions, chopped
1 tsp. fresh grated gingerroot
1 clove garlic, pressed
1 tsp. ground cumin
1 tsp. ground coriander
½ tsp. turmeric
½ tsp. garam masala
  (recipe in volume I)

⅛ tsp. cayenne (optional)
2 tomatoes, cut in chunks
4 cups cooked chopped potatoes
  (4-5 potatoes)
1½ cups frozen green peas
  (thawed)
2-3 tbsp. chopped fresh coriander

In a Silverstone frying pan, heat ½ cup water. Add onions, gingerroot and garlic. Saute for a few minutes until onions soften slightly, then add spices and ⅓ cup more water. Cook and stir over high heat for several minutes. Remove from heat. Place in blender jar with ⅛ cup water. Process until smooth. Pour into saucepan. Add 1 cup water and the tomatoes. Cook over medium heat for 10 minutes. Add the potatoes and peas. Cook an additional 10 minutes.

Remove from heat. Garnish with coriander before serving.

Serve over brown rice or rolled up in a chapati.

# TVP STUFFING MIX

### SERVINGS: 8-10

PREPARATION TIME: 15 mins.    COOKING TIME: 30 mins.

3 cups tofu TVP (recipe found in
  Volume I)
1 large onion, chopped
½ cup celery, chopped
½ cup currants

½ cup cooked beans (garbanzo,
white, pinto, or kidney)
2 cups tomato sauce

Saute onion and celery in ⅓ cup water until translucent. Stir in the TVP and cook a few minutes. Add the currants, beans and tomato sauce. Mix well. Add remaining seasonings from options list under helpful hints. Simmer over low heat about 20-25 minutes.

HELPFUL HINTS: This stuffing mix can be made with a variety of seasonings, depending on what flavors you like.

MEXICAN:
2½ tbsp. chili powder
¼ cup chopped black
olives (optional)

ITALIAN:
1 tsp. basil
1 tsp. oregano
1 tbsp. parsley flakes

FRENCH:
½ tsp. thyme
½ tsp. rosemary
½ tsp. marjoram
1 tbsp. red wine
(optional)

ORIENTAL:
½ tsp. powdered ginger
½ tsp. dry mustard
1 tbsp. low sodium soy sauce
1 tbsp. Sherry (optional)

GREEK:
½ tsp. cinnamon
½ tsp. ground cumin
1 tbsp. lemon juice
dash black pepper

INDIAN:
1 tsp. turmeric
1 tsp. ground coriander
1 tsp. ground cumin
dash black pepper

This mixture may be used to stuff many different foods. Try it in chapatis, pita, or corn tortillas with a variety of toppings or sauces. You may also use it to stuff various vegetables, such as green peppers, eggplants, zucchini, or tomatoes. To prepare vegetables, cut off their tops, scoop out the insides (reserve for other uses), fill with mixture, place in a baking dish, add ½ inch water to the dish, bake at 350 degrees for 30-45 minutes. Also see recipe for Stuffed Chapati Rolls in this volume.

# Vegetable Side Dishes

*Contributed by Jim O'Keefe*
## JIM'S BREADED EGGPLANT

### SERVINGS: 8

PREPARATION TIME: 10 mins.    COOKING TIME: 20 mins.

2 eggplants, large, sliced in ½"
  rounds
2 (15 oz.) cans tomato sauce
2 tsp. basil (or 1½ tsp. oregano)

1 pkg. (1.3 oz.) Hain onion soup
  mix
1 cup corn meal
½ cup unprocessed bran
½ cup brown rice flour

Slice eggplant (do not peel). Combine tomato sauce, basil and soup mix in a bowl and mix well. In another bowl, combine corn meal, bran and rice flour for breading. Using tongs, dip a slice of eggplant in the tomato sauce mixture until coated. Then bread the eggplant by holding it above the breading bowl and spooning the breading mixture quickly over both sides. Place the breaded eggplant on a non-stick baking sheet. Bake in a preheated 400 degree oven for 20 minutes, or until it is tender and brown.

HELPFUL HINTS: This breading method also works well with other vegetables, such as sliced yellow onions and whole mushrooms. It is good for snacks and also freezes well.

## COLCANNON

SERVINGS: 6

PREPARATION TIME: 45 mins.    COOKING TIME: 30 mins.

8 medium potatoes                       1 bunch green onions, chopped
1 small head cabbage

Peel and chop potatoes, boil until tender. Drain, reserve water. Mash until smooth, using some of the reserved water as liquid.

Shred the cabbage. Saute in a small amount of water until limp, about 10 minutes.

Stir cabbage and green onions into mashed potatoes. Sprinkle with some black pepper and paprika.

Bake at 350 degrees for 30 minutes.

## ITALIAN CAULIFLOWER

SERVINGS: 4-6

PREPARATION TIME: 15 mins.    COOKING TIME: 10-15 mins.

2 lbs. cauliflower, cut into             ⅓ cup oil-free Italian dressing
  flowerettes

Steam cauliflower over 1 inch of boiling water about 10-15 minutes or until tender. Drain. Place cauliflower in bowl. Pour dressing over, toss gently to mix. May be served hot or cold.

## DEVILED GREEN BEANS

SERVINGS: 6

PREPARATION TIME: 15 mins.    COOKING TIME: 10 mins.

| | |
|---|---|
| 1 lb. fresh green beans | 2 tbsp. vinegar |
| 1 cup water | 2 tsp. Dijon mustard |

Clean beans and cut into 1 inch pieces. Cook in the water until tender, about 10 minutes. Drain off water, reserving 3 tbsp. Mix reserved water, vinegar and mustard. Pour over green beans. Stir until well coated. Serve hot or cold.

HELPFUL HINTS: 20 oz. of frozen green beans may be substituted for fresh, if desired.

## MEXICAN CORN

### SERVINGS: 4-6

PREPARATION TIME: 10 mins.    COOKING TIME: 20 mins.

| | |
|---|---|
| 1 small onion, chopped | ¼ cup canned chopped green |
| 1 clove garlic, crushed | chilies |
| 2 tomatoes, chopped | several dashes Tabasco sauce |
| 4 cups frozen corn kernels | chopped fresh coriander for garnish (optional) |

Saute onions and garlic in a small amount of water in a saucepan until soft, about 5 minutes. Add tomatoes, corn, green chilies and Tabasco sauce. Cook, covered, over medium-low heat for 15 minutes. Stir occasionally. Garnish with coriander, if desired, before serving.

*Contributed by Gordon Tang*

## UNFORGETTABLE CHINESE EGGPLANT

### SERVINGS: 6

PREPARATION TIME: 15 mins.    COOKING TIME: 20-25 mins.

| | |
|---|---|
| 4 medium long eggplants | 2 tbsp. low sodium soy sauce |
| 4 cloves garlic, crushed | ¼ tsp. crushed red chili pepper |
| 1 thumb-size piece of gingerroot | (optional) |
| 2 stalks green onions | |

Cut eggplant into ½ by 1 inch pieces. Cook in a small amount of boiling water until almost done (5-8 minutes). Drain.

Slice ginger, garlic and green onions into ¹⁄₁₆ inch slivers.
Saute ginger and garlic in 1 tbsp. water for about 2 minutes on high heat.
Add eggplant and continue to cook for a few minutes.
Add soy sauce, green onions (and optional chili pepper, if desired.) Cook until done, the softer the better.

Serve with brown rice.

## BROILED DIJON TOMATOES

### SERVINGS: 4

PREPARATION TIME: 10 mins.    COOKING TIME: 3-4 mins.

4 tomatoes, cut in half            ¼ tsp. dry mustard
2 cloves garlic, pressed           ½ tsp. water
1 tbsp. Dijon mustard

In a small bowl, combine the garlic, Dijon mustard and dry mustard. Add the water, a little at a time, stirring as you do so. Put the tomatoes on a broiling pan and spread the mustard mixture over them. Broil the tomatoes under a preheated broiler (about 3 inches from heat) for 3-4 minutes until bubbly. Watch them carefully.

## QUICK ORIENTAL CABBAGE

### SERVINGS: 4

PREPARATION TIME: 10 mins.    COOKING TIME: 10 mins.

6 cups coarsely chopped cabbage      2 tbsp. low sodium soy sauce
½ cup water                          1 tbsp. rice vinegar

Place all ingredients in a pot with a tight fitting lid. Bring to a boil and cook over medium heat for 10 minutes, stirring occasionally.

HELPFUL HINTS: To spice this up a little, try adding a dash or two (or more) of Tabasco sauce with the other seasonings.

## POTATO-ONION BAKE

### SERVINGS: 6

PREPARATION TIME: 15 mins.    COOKING TIME: 1¼ hrs.

| | |
|---|---|
| 4 medium salad potatoes | 2 cups water |
| 1 onion | 3 tbsp. low sodium soy sauce |

Scrub potatoes, do not peel. Slice very thin. Slice onion very thin. Alternate potato and onion slices in a baking dish. Heat water; add soy sauce. Pour over potatoes and onions. Cover.
Bake at 375 degrees for 1¼ hrs.

## ZUCCHINI CASSEROLE

### SERVINGS: 6

PREPARATION TIME: 15 mins.    COOKING TIME: 30 mins.

| | |
|---|---|
| 4 cups sliced zucchini | ½ tsp. oregano |
| 1 onion, thinly sliced | 1 tsp. basil |
| 1 (4 oz.) jar chopped pimiento | 1 (15-16 oz.) can tomato sauce |

Slice the zucchini about ¼ inch thick. Lay in the bottom of a medium sized oblong baking dish. Separate onion into rings and lay over zucchini. Next spoon the pimiento over the top of the onions and zucchini. Sprinkle herbs over this, then pour the tomato sauce over it all. Cover baking dish with foil. Bake at 375 degrees for 30 minutes.

## SAUTEED MUSHROOMS

### SERVINGS: 2-4

PREPARATION TIME: 10 mins.    COOKING TIME: 10 mins.

| | |
|---|---|
| 1 large onion, chopped or sliced | ½ cup white wine |
| ½ lb. mushrooms, thickly sliced | 2 cloves garlic, crushed |

Place all ingredients in a saucepan. Saute over medium heat about 10 minutes, until mushrooms are tender but not mushy.

HELPFUL HINTS: Serve plain or as a topping for baked potatoes, acorn squash or whole grains. May also be made without the onions. Cut the mushrooms in half or leave whole. Proceed as directed above.

## STEAMED GREENS

### SERVINGS: 2-4

PREPARATION TIME: 10-15 mins.    COOKING TIME: 15 mins.

1 large onion, thinly sliced
10-12 cups finely shredded
  or chopped leafy greens
(kale, collards, chard, mustard
  greens, escarole, etc.)

lemon juice
Tabasco sauce (optional)

Place a small amount of water in a large pan (with a lid). Add onion, saute a few minutes, then add greens, and saute until just wilted. Cover and steam about 10 minutes. Stir occasionally. Sprinkle with some fresh lemon juice. Add a dash or two of Tabasco if desired.

HELPFUL HINTS: These can be shredded very quickly if you have a food processor. (Use slicing blade). Prepare greens and onions ahead of time. Store in plastic bag.

*Contributed by the McGoldricks*
## GINGER CARROTS

SERVINGS: 4

PREPARATION TIME: 10 mins.    COOKING TIME: 15 mins.

5 large carrots, sliced
½ inch piece of gingerroot, grated

½ orange rind, grated
1 tbsp. honey

Cook carrots in ½ inch of water until tender (about 15 minutes). Add ginger, orange rind and honey. Stir well. Serve hot.

## GNOCCHI

SERVINGS: 6-8

PREPARATION TIME: 45 mins.    COOKING TIME: variable

4 medium potatoes              1⅓ cup unbleached flour

Peel the potatoes, cut into large chunks and cook until tender. Drain and mash with a potato masher. Mix in the flour and knead until the mixture is smooth. Shape the dough into long rolls about ½ inch in diameter. Cut dough into 1 inch pieces, now called gnocchi.

Drop the gnocchi into boiling water a few at a time. When they rise to the surface remove with a slotted spoon. Place in a casserole dish with a lid to keep warm. Serve with a sauce to cover them, such as a Marinara Sauce, Mushroom gravy, Spicy Gravy (recipes all found in the McDougall Cookbooks) or one of your families favorites.

# CAJUN POTATOES

### SERVINGS: 4

PREPARATION TIME: Time: 10 mins.    COOKING TIME: 20 mins.

2 lbs. new potatoes
2 tbsp. Cajun spices (recipe in this
   volume)

3 cups water

Scrub potatoes and leave whole. Place potatoes, spices and water in a sauce-pan. Bring to a boil, cover and cook for 15-20 minutes until potatoes are tender. Do not let them get mushy.

HELPFUL HINTS: If you cannot find new potatoes, then use white potatoes which you have scrubbed and cut into chunks. Follow the same instructions as above. For a spicier version, remove cover for the last 10 minutes of cooking and let some of the water evaporate, leaving the spices coating the potatoes.

## SWEET POTATOES AND APRICOTS

### SERVINGS: 12

PREPARATION TIME: 20 mins.    COOKING TIME: 45 mins.
(cooked sweet potatoes needed)

2½ lbs. sweet potatoes, cooked,
   peeled, and cut into large pieces
1 cup chopped dried apricots
¾ cup orange juice

½ cup water
4 tbsp. honey
½ cup walnut pieces (optional)

Prepare sweet potatoes as directed above. Place apricots, orange juice, water, and honey in a saucepan. Bring to a boil. Reduce heat, cover, and simmer until apricots are soft, about 25-30 minutes. Remove from heat.

Arrange sweet potatoes in a baking dish. Sprinkle with walnuts, if desired. Pour apricot sauce over the top. Cover. Bake at 350 degrees until heated, about 15-20 minutes.

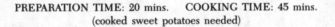

*Contributed by Linda and Milton DuPuy*

## MASHED STUFFED SQUASH

### SERVINGS: 8

PREPARATION TIME: 45 mins.    COOKING TIME: 1¼ hrs.

2 medium acorn squash
2 medium carrots, chopped
2 small turnips, chopped
1 tbsp. maple syrup

½ tsp. cinnamon
¼ tsp. nutmeg
1 cup coarsely shredded, peeled
  apple

Cut squash in half and clean out seeds. Place cut side down in a baking dish. Cover with foil. Bake at 350 degrees for 30 minutes. Turn cut side up, bake for 30 minutes longer. Scoop pulp out of each half, keeping shells intact. Place cooked pulp in bowl and set aside.

Meanwhile, place carrots and turnips in water and cook, covered, for 20 minutes or until tender. Drain. Add to cooked squash. Beat by hand or electric mixer until mashed. Stir in maple syrup, cinnamon and nutmeg. Then add apples. Mix well. Spoon mixture into squash shells. Bake uncovered at 350 degrees for 15 minutes.

## *Contributed by Jennifer Tyson*
## LEMON BROCCOLI

SERVINGS: 6-8

PREPARATION TIME: 10 mins.     COOKING TIME: 15 mins.

1 bunch broccoli
1 large lemon

2 tsp. garlic powder

Wash broccoli and peel the tough outer skin from the thickest part of the stalks with a knife. Slice the stalks into ¼" circles and cut the rest of the head into flowerets. Put one inch of water in a large pot and insert vegetable steamer. Put broccoli in steamer basket, cover and bring to a boil. Steam until broccoli is barely fork tender and still bright green. Drain off water, remove steamer basket, and spread broccoli in bottom of pot. Cut lemon into quarters lengthwise. Squeeze the lemon pieces over the hot broccoli, pressing out as much juice as possible. Throw the pieces of squeezed lemon into the pot. Sprinkle the broccoli with garlic powder, cover the pan again, and allow broccoli to absorb the flavors for 10 minutes.

HELPFUL HINTS: If you prefer, you can use four cloves of crushed fresh garlic instead of the garlic powder. This dish is delicious either hot or cold.

## *Contributed by Elaine French*
## GOURMET CROOKNECK SQUASH

SERVINGS: 6-8

PREPARATION TIME: 10 mins.     COOKING TIME: 15 mins.

3 yellow crookneck squash          1½ tsp. dill weed
1½ cups orange juice

Slice squash into ½" circles and place in a saucepan. Add orange juice and dill weed. Bring to a boil, then reduce heat and simmer until squash is tender but still firm (10-15 minutes).

HELPFUL HINTS: This is a nice side dish for a holiday meal. Try using carrots instead of squash.

## SEASONED POTATOES IN FOIL

SERVINGS: 4-6

PREPARATION TIME: 10-20 mins.    COOKING TIME: 45-50 mins.

6 large white potatoes          1 medium onion

Wash potatoes. Peel if you wish, and slice into ⅛ inch slices. Slice onion thinly and separate into rings. Place potatoes on a large sheet of foil wrap. Lay onions over potatoes. Season with a few sprinkles of low sodium soy sauce, some black pepper and a little paprika, if desired. Fold foil up over the vegetables and seal edges securely. Place on a baking sheet and bake in a 350 degree oven for 45-50 minutes.

HELPFUL HINTS: Other seasonings can be used as desired—choose your favorites. This can be cooked on a grill at a cookout.

*Contributed by Ben Nichols*

## MANDARIN EGGPLANT

SERVINGS: 4

PREPARATION TIME: 30 mins.    COOKING TIME: 20-25 mins.

1-2 lbs. eggplant                    3 tbsp. low sodium soy sauce
2 large onions, sliced               2 tsp. honey
1 carrot, sliced                     2 tbsp. rice vinegar
4 cloves garlic, crushed             2 tbsp. cornstarch
1 cup water                          1 tbsp. acceptable ketchup or
¼ tsp. ground chili powder              tomato puree
8 drops Tabasco sauce                1 tbsp. grated fresh gingerroot

Peel eggplant and cut into ⅜ inch strips. Saute eggplant with onions, carrots, and garlic in a wok or saucepan with a small amount of water and cook until tender, about 10-15 minutes.

Place ½ cup water in a separate sauce pan. Add chili powder, Tabasco sauce, soy sauce, honey, rice vinegar, and Ketchup. Mix well. Cook over medium heat. Mix cornstarch with the remaining ½ cup water until smooth. Slowly add to the mixture in the sauce pan stirring constantly. Now add the grated gingerroot. Cook and stir until mixture boils and thickens. Pour over the eggplant mixture and stir gently. Heat thoroughly.

Serve with brown rice or steamed whole wheat rolls or manapua (recipe found elsewhere in this book).

## SAUCY BRUSSELS SPROUTS

SERVINGS: 4

PREPARATION TIME: 15 mins.    COOKING TIME: 15-20 mins.

1½ lbs. fresh Brussels Sprouts       ⅓ cup oil-free Italian dressing
½ lb. cherry tomatoes
   or 2 tomatoes cut in wedges

Prepare Brussels Sprouts by removing any discolored leaves. Cut off·stem ends and wash. Steam over 1 inch boiling water about 10-15 minutes until tender. Remove steamer basket and drain out water. Place Brussels Sprouts back in pan, add tomatoes, and dressing. Toss to mix. Cover and let rest for 5 minutes to warm tomatoes and dressing. May be served hot or cold.

*Contributed by Neil Orenstein PhD*
## CRISPY YAM TREAT

SERVINGS: variable

PREPARATION TIME: 15 mins.    COOKING TIME: 1½ hrs.

yams-choose the amount you want
   to prepare

Bake the yams in a 350 degree oven until tender. Remove from oven and cool. Slice the yams into ⅜ inch thick slices. Bake these slices on a teflon coated baking sheet for 30 to 40 minutes in a 250 degree oven. The longer you bake the slices the more crispy they will be; the less time you bake the slices the more moist they will be. Bake to taste and enjoy.

# GREEN BEAN SPECIAL

SERVINGS: 6

PREPARATION TIME: 20 mins.    COOKING TIME: 20 mins.

1½ lbs. green beans
1 onion, thinly sliced
½ tsp. turmeric
1 clove garlic, pressed
1 tsp. grated fresh gingerroot

1 tomato, chopped
2 tsp. low sodium soy sauce
2 tsp. lemon juice
2 dashes Tabasco sauce
1-2 tbsp. chopped fresh coriander

Clean green beans and cut or slice as desired. Cook in boiling water for 15 minutes. Drain. Rinse under cool water. Drain and set aside.

Cook the onion in ¼ cup water until soft. Add turmeric. Cook and stir for a minute. Then add garlic, gingerroot, tomatoes, soy sauce, Tabasco, and lemon juice. Cook over low heat about 10 minutes. Add the beans. Mix well. Cook an additional 5 minutes. Sprinkle with coriander before serving.

# INDIA EGGPLANT

SERVINGS: 4

PREPARATION TIME: 45 mins. for eggplant    COOKING TIME: 25 mins.
15 mins. remaining

1 large eggplant or 2 smallish ones
1 onion, sliced
½ tsp. cumin seeds
½ tbsp. grated fresh ginger root
1 green pepper, chopped
1 tomato, chopped
1 tsp. turmeric

2 tsp. ground coriander
1 tsp. ground cumin
1 tsp. paprika
¼ tsp. pepper (optional)
¾ cup water
¼ cup chopped fresh coriander

Prick eggplant in several places with a fork. Place in baking dish. Bake at 400 degrees for 45 minutes or until soft. Cool. Cut in half, scoop out insides and chop the pulp. Set aside.

In a medium saucepan, place ¼ cup water, the onion, cumin seed and ginger. Saute until onion is soft, about 5 minutes.

Add green pepper, tomato, turmeric, ground coriander, cumin, paprika (and optional pepper). Cook an additional 5 minutes. Add the remaining water, bring to a boil, reduce heat and simmer for 10 minutes. Add the chopped eggplant. Cook an additional 5 minutes. Stir in the chopped coriander just before serving.

# ZUCCHINI-POTATO CURRY

SERVINGS: 6

PREPARATION TIME: 15 mins.    COOKING TIME: 35 mins.

1 onion, chopped
½ tsp. turmeric
1 tsp. garam masala (recipe in volume I)
2 medium potatoes, cut into ½ inch cubes

4 zucchini, chopped into ½ inch chunks
1 tomato, chopped
¼ cup chopped fresh coriander

Saute onion in ¼ cup water for 5 minutes. Add turmeric and garam masala. Stir to mix. Add potatoes and ¼ cup water. Stir. Cover and simmer over medium heat for 15 minutes. Add zucchini and another ¼ cup water. Cover and continue to simmer for 10-15 minutes. Add tomato and coriander. Mix well. Cover and cook 3-5 minutes longer. May be served hot or cold.

# ONION BAKED APPLES

SERVINGS: 4-6

PREPARATION TIME: 15 mins.    COOKING TIME: 15 mins.

2 onions, sliced and separated into rings
3 apples (Delicious are preferable)
3 tbsp. honey
½ tsp. cinnamon

⅛ tsp. ground cloves
⅛ tsp. allspice
½ tsp. fresh grated orange rind

Place onions in a pan with ½ cup water. Cook over medium heat, stirring often until onions are soft, about 10 minutes. Add remaining ingredients, except for the orange rind. Cook and stir until apples soften slightly, about 5 minutes. Stir in orange rind. Serve warm.

# Desserts

## EASY CAROB CAKE

SERVINGS: makes 8 inch square cake

PREPARATION TIME: 15 mins.    COOKING TIME: 30 mins.

| | |
|---|---|
| 2 cups whole wheat pastry flour | ¾ cup honey |
| 4 tbsp. carob powder | 5 tbsp. applesauce |
| 1 tsp. baking soda | 1 tbsp. vinegar |
| ½ tsp baking powder | 1 tsp. vanilla |
| 1 cup warm water | |

Combine dry ingredients in a large bowl. Combine wet ingredients in a separate bowl. Pour wet ingredients into dry ingredients and mix well. Pour into non-stick 8 inch square pan. Bake at 350 degrees for 30 minutes.

# FRUIT ICES

SERVINGS: 4-6

PREPARATION TIME: 15 mins.    CHILLING TIME: 2 hrs.

I.  2 cups papaya puree
    1 cup water
    2 tbsp. lemon juice
    2 tbsp. honey

II. 2 cups honeydew puree
    1 cup frozen blueberries

III. 2 cups Kiwi puree
    1 cup water
    1 tbsp. lemon juice
    4 tbsp. honey

IV. 4 cups seeded and chopped watermelon
    ½ cup water
    1 tbsp. lemon juice
    4 tbsp. honey

Combine all ingredients from chosen preparation above (I-IV). Process briefly in blender until smooth. Pour into a bowl or shallow pan. Place in the freezer. Stir or beat the mixture every 15 minutes to break up ice crystals. It will be ready to serve in about 2 hours.

HELPFUL HINTS: These ices taste best when they are prepared and served after the initial 2 hours of chilling time. If the ice happens to freeze solid, break up and place in the blender again and process briefly. Freeze or serve at once.

These may also be prepared in an electric ice cream freezer.

# FRUIT PUDDING

SERVINGS: 6-8

PREPARATION TIME: 15 mins. CHILLING TIME: 2 hrs.

1½ lbs. tofu
1 10 oz. pkg. frozen berries,
   thawed and drained
(raspberries or strawberries)

1 banana, mashed
¼ cup honey
2 tbsp. lemon juice
1½ tsp. vanilla

Place all ingredients in a blender and process until smooth. Chill for at least 2 hours. Serve very cold.

# TAPIOCA

SERVINGS: 8

PREPARATION TIME: 15 mins.   COOKING TIME: 5 mins.
CHILLING TIME: 2 hrs.

3 tbsp. instant tapioca
2½ cups water
6 oz. frozen apple or
   orange juice concentrate

3 ½ cups fresh fruit,
   cut in bite-size pieces
(melons, oranges, peaches, bananas,
   etc)

Combine tapioca and 1 cup of the water in a saucepan. Bring to a boil and simmer for 5 minutes. Add remaining water and frozen juice concentrate, mix until well blended. Cover and chill for at least 1 hour. Then add prepared fruit to the tapioca mixture. Mix lightly. Cover and chill again before serving.

# APPLE PIE FILLING

SERVINGS: fills one piecrust

PREPARATION TIME: 30 mins.   COOKING TIME: 60 mins.

6 cups peeled, sliced apples
1 tbsp. lemon juice
¼ cup honey

2 tbsp. whole wheat pastry flour
½ tsp. cinnamon
¼ tsp. nutmeg

Combine the apples with the lemon juce. Mix in the honey and toss gently until coated. Mix flour, cinnamon and nutmeg. Add to apples and toss again to mix. Place into an unbaked pie crust.

Sprinkle with a few raisins or Grapenuts, if desired.

Bake at 375 degrees for 30 minutes. Reduce heat to 325 degrees and bake an additional 30 minutes.

## NUTTY PIE CRUST

SERVINGS: Makes 1 crust

PREPARATION TIME: 15 mins.    COOKING TIME: 15 mins. unfilled
40-50 mins. filled

¾ cup cashews                               ¾ cup whole wheat pastry flour
⅓ cup water

Place cashews and water in blender jar. Process until smooth. Transfer to a bowl. Add pastry flour, mix well. Press into a pie pan with fingers. (Moisten fingers with water to keep dough from sticking to them.)

Use either unbaked or fill and bake according to filling directions. OR Bake unfilled: bake at 375 degrees for 10-15 minutes.

HELPFUL HINTS: For best results, use a non-stick pie plate or a lightly oiled pie plate.

*Contributed by Bess McGladrey*

## PUMPKIN PIE

SERVINGS: 1 pie

PREPARATION TIME: 15 mins.    COOKING TIME: 35 mins.

CRUST:

1 cup Grape Nuts cereal                ¼ cup frozen apple juice
                                       concentrate

FILLING:

1 (16 oz.) can pumpkin          1 tsp. cinnamon
8 oz. firm tofu                 ½ tsp. ground ginger
⅓ cup honey                     ¼ tsp. ground cloves
2 tbsp. whole wheat pastry flour   1 tsp. vanilla

Thaw the apple juice concentrate. Crush the Grape Nuts with a rolling pin or in a blender. Combine these two ingredients and pat into a 9 inch pie pan.

Place all other ingredients in a blender jar or food processor and process until very smooth. Pour into crust. Bake at 325 degrees for 35 minutes.

*Contributed by Elaine French*
## PEANUT BUTTER COOKIES
SERVINGS: 48 cookies

PREPARATION TIME: 20 mins.    COOKING TIME: 15 mins.

3 cups whole wheat flour
½ cup soy flour
1 tsp. baking powder
½ tsp. baking soda

½ cup applesauce
½ cup water
¾ cup honey
¾ cup peanut butter

In a medium size bowl, mix flours, baking powder and soda. In a large bowl, mix applesauce, water, honey and peanut butter until smooth. Add flour mixture to peanut butter mixture and mix well. Drop by tablespoonfuls onto cookie sheet. Flatten with fork dipped in flour. Bake at 300 degrees for 15 minutes.

## PEACH PIE FILLING

SERVINGS: fills 1 piecrust

PREPARATION TIME: 30 mins.    COOKING TIME: 45 mins.

6 cups peeled sliced peaches
3 tbsp. whole wheat pastry flour
⅓ cup honey

1 tbsp. lemon juice
¼ tsp. cinnamon

Place sliced peaches in a large bowl. Sprinkle with the flour, mix gently to coat well. Mix in remaining ingredients. Place in unbaked piecrust. Sprinkle with a few Grapenuts, if desired.

Bake at 375 degrees for 30 minutes. Reduce heat to 350 degrees and bake an additional 15 minutes.

*Contributed by John Ware*
## WHOLE WHEAT CREPE

SERVINGS: makes 20-24 crepes

PREPARATION TIME: 5 mins.    COOKING TIME: variable

| | |
|---|---|
| 1¼ cups whole wheat flour | 2 cups water |
| 2 tbsp. arrowroot | |

Blend ingredients. Heat a very lightly oiled crepe pan until it just starts to smoke. Pour in 2 ounces of batter and move pan around until it is evenly coated with batter. When crepe edges curl, flip with spatula and cook 30 seconds more. Set aside. Do the same with all remaining batter. Stack crepes between sheets of waxed paper.

Use with fruit filling for dessert or a vegetable filling for a main dish.

HELPFUL HINTS: To make a simple fruit sauce follow directions: Blend 8 oz. unsweetened applesauce, 3 oz. fresh pineapple and a pinch of cinnamon. Place in saucepan with 1 cup sliced apple, ½ cup raisins, a pinch of nutmeg, and a pinch of ground cloves. Simmer for 5 minutes. Roll mixture in the crepe.

## OKARA COOKIES

SERVINGS: 48 cookies

PREPARATION TIME: 20 mins.    COOKING TIME: 12 mins.

| | |
|---|---|
| 1 cup whole wheat flour | 1 cup honey |
| 3 cups rolled oats | ½ cup applesauce |
| 1 tsp. baking soda | 1 tsp. vanilla |
| 2 cups okara | |

Combine flour, oats, and baking soda in a bowl. Combine okara, honey, applesauce, and vanilla in another bowl. Add moist ingredients to dry ingredients and mix well. Then mix in 1 cup of your choice: raisins, date pieces, carob chips, etc. Form into cookie-sized patties in your hands and place each one on a cookie sheet ( it is not necessary to leave much space between these). Bake at 350 degrees for 12 minutes.

HELPFUL HINTS: Store in an airtight container in the refrigerator.

Okara is a by-product of tofu making. It is the pulp that is left behind after the soymilk has been pressed from the soybean. It is white in color and very high in fiber.

## OATMEAL DESSERT

SERVINGS: 6-8

PREPARTAION TIME: 15 mins.    COOKING TIME: 60 mins.

2 cups rolled oats
4 cups water
½ cup raisins
1 tbsp. vanilla
⅛ tsp. mace

⅛ tsp. ground coriander
2 cups sliced peaches—fresh or
  canned in their own juice

Combine the first six ingredients in a 2 quart casserole, mixing well. Arrange the peaches over the top. Bake uncovered at 350 degrees for 1 hour. Let rest for 15 minutes before serving.

*Contributed by Phyllis Browne and Priscilla Brockway*
## "CHOCOLATE" BANANA ICE CREAM

### SERVINGS: 8

### PREPARATION TIME: 20 mins. CHILLING TIME: 2-3 hrs.

1 cup apple juice concentrate
1 cup apple juice
3 tbsp. brown rice flour
½ cup carob powder

2 tbsp. tahini
2 tbsp. maple syrup
4 ripe bananas

Combine juice and concentrate in a saucepan. Blend in rice flour and carob powder. Bring to a boil, stirring constantly. Pour into blender or food processor and blend with remaining ingredients. Chill well and freeze.

See freezing directions under Strawberry Ice Cream.

*Contributed by Phyllis Browne and Pricilla Brockway*
## STRAWBERRY ICE CREAM

### SERVINGS: 8

### PREPARATION TIME: 20 mins. CHILING TIME: 2-3 hrs.

1 cup frozen apple juice
  concentrate
1 cup apple juice
2 tbsp. arrowroot
2 tbsp. tahini

2 to 3 tbsp. honey
2 cups fresh or frozen strawberries
2 tsp. vanilla

Combine the juice and the concentrate in a saucepan. Blend in the arrowroot. Cook until thickened, stirring constantly. Place in blender or food processor and blend with remaining ingredients. Chill well and freeze.

HELPFUL HINTS: These may be frozen in an electric ice cream freezer or in the refrigerator-freezer. Pour mixture in a shallow metal tray. Freeze for 1 to 2 hours, until edges are firm, but center is still slushy. Then stir well, and return to freezer for an additional hour. Remove from freezer and process in a food processor until smooth (or beat with electric mixer.) Pour into plastic container and freeze for several more hours.

*Contributed by Neil Orenstein PhD.*

## ACCIDENTAL MOUSSE

SERVINGS: 4

PREPARATION TIME: 15 mins.    COOKING TIME: none

6 very ripe bananas
1½ cups unsweetened applesauce

2 tbsp. carob powder
¼ tsp. vanilla extract

Blend the applesauce and the bananas in a food processor using the steel blade. (Cut the bananas into quarters and add them to the blending applesauce one piece at a time.) Add carob powder and vanilla extract. Continue to blend until the mixture is smooth and all of the bananas have been blended with no chunks remaining. Spoon into individual dessert cups. Refrigerate for 30 minutes before serving.

*Contributed by Janice Morikawa*

## BANANA-RAISIN COOKIES

SERVINGS: 16-18 cookies

PREPARATION TIME: 25 mins.    COOKING TIME: 15 mins.

2 ripe bananas, mashed
1¼ cups rolled oats
1 cup whole wheat flour
½ tsp. baking soda
½ tsp. baking powder

1 tsp. cinnamon
½ cup raisins
1 tsp. vanilla
½ cup apple juice or water

Preheat oven to 375 degrees. Combine all the dry ingredients in a large bowl. Add the remaining ingredients and mix well. (Batter should be a little stiff.) Drop by teaspoon on to a non-stick cookie sheet and flatten slightly. Bake at 375 degrees for 15 minutes. Store in an air-tight container.

*Contributed by Janine Shrader*

## CARROT CAKE

SERVINGS: 13 x 9 inch cake

PREPARATION TIME: 40 mins.    COOKING TIME: 1 hr.

2 cups whole wheat flour
3/4 cups honey
1 1/4 cups applesauce
4 tsp. egg replacer, well mixed in 8 tbsp. water
1 1/2 tsp. baking soda
2 tsp. baking powder
2 tsp. cinnamon

1/2 tsp. nutmeg
1/2 tsp. cloves
1/2 tsp. allspice
3 cups grated carrots
1 (8 oz.) can pineapple, crushed (slightly drained)
1/2 cup raisins
1 cup chopped walnuts (optional)

Mix dry ingredients together (flour, spices, baking soda and powder). Add honey, applesauce and mixed egg replacer. Mix well. Add carrots, pineapple, raisins and nuts. Stir well. Turn into a non-stick baking pan 13x9x2 inches. Bake at 350 degrees for 1 hour.

HELPFUL HINTS: If you do not have a non-stick baking dish, you will have to lightly oil and flour your pan.

*Contributed by Ben Nichols*

## APPLE BRAN CAKE

SERVINGS: makes an 8 inch square cake

PREPARATION TIME: 20 mins.    COOKING TIME: 40-50 mins.

2 cups whole wheat flour
2 cups bran
2 tsp. egg replacer (optional)
1 tsp. allspice
1 tsp. cinnamon
1/2 tsp. ground cloves
1/2 tsp. powdered ginger

2 tsp. baking powder
1 cup honey
1 cup peeled, diced apples
1/2 cup applesauce
1/2 cup water
1/2 cup raisins (optional)
1/2 tsp. vanilla

Mix dry ingredients together. Mix moist ingredients together. Add flour mixture to moist ingredients. Stir gently until well mixed. Turn into a square non-stick baking pan. Bake at 350 degrees for 40-50 minutes until cake pulls away from side of pan.

HELPFUL HINTS: This may also be made in a muffin tin. Other fruit can be substituted for the apples, such as bananas.

*Contributed by Chef Teruya of the Outrigger Canoe Club*

## POACHED PEARS

SERVINGS: 6

PREPARATION TIME: 45 mins.     COOKING TIME: 30 mins.
CHILLING TIME: 2 hrs.

PEARS:

6 pears, pared
2 cups chablis
2 cups water
1 cinnamon stick

2 cloves
1½ cups honey
zest and juice of ½ orange
zest and juice of ½ lemon

Prepare pears. Bring other ingredients to a boil in a large saucepan. Add pears. Poach about 30 minutes, or until tender. Pierce with a skewer or a fork. Cool in liquid, then remove from liquid and chill.

SAUCE:

1 lb. fresh strawberries, cleaned
6 tbsp. honey

1 tbsp. fresh orange juice
small amount water as needed

Puree sauce in blender.

TO SERVE: Place a pear on an individual serving plate. Pour a little sauce over pear. Garnish with orange segments and mint leaves. Repeat with all pears.

HELPFUL HINTS: Apple juice may be substituted for the chablis.

This makes a beautiful, elegant dessert, well worth your efforts for a celebration meal.

## ORANGE BAKED APPLES

SERVINGS: 4

PREPARATION TIME: 10 mins.     COOKING TIME: 1 hr.

4 large apples
2 tsp. honey

1 cup orange juice

Peel the top half of the apples. Cut out blossom end and stem end. Place in individual baking dishes. Place ½ tsp. honey in top indentation of apple. Pour scant ¼ cup orange juice over apple into each dish. Bake at 350 degrees for 60 minutes. Serve slightly warm or at room temperature.

## BERRY SORBET

SERVINGS: makes 1 qt.

PREPARATION TIME: 15 mins. CHILLING TIME: 3 hrs.

1 cup water
½ cup honey
4 cups frozen strawberries or
raspberries

2 tbsp. lemon juice

In a small saucepan, combine the water and honey. Bring to a boil. Stir. Remove from heat. Cool. In a blender or food processor, blend berries until smooth. Add lemon juice and water-honey mixture. Process briefly. Pour into bowl. Cover and freeze until slushy. Beat with electric mixer until smooth again. Return to bowl and freeze until firm. Let stand at room temperature 5-10 minutes before serving.

## GRAPENUTS DESSERT TOPPING

SERVINGS: covers 1 pie

PREPARATION TIME: 5 mins. COOKING TIME: 5-10 mins.

1 cup Grapenuts cereal
1½ tbsp. apple juice concentrate

2 tsp. vanilla

Place Grapenuts in blender jar and process briefly. Combine crushed Grapenuts with remaining ingredients. Mix well. Spread on a baking sheet and bake at 300 degrees until crispy, about 5-10 minutes. Use as a topping for apple crisp, apple or peach pie or other dessert. May also be used without baking. Just spoon directly on the dessert and bake as directed.

*Contributed by Carol Kukea*

## CAROL'S APPLE CRISP

SERVINGS: fills small baking dish

PREPARATION TIME: 20 mins.    COOKING TIME: 15 mins.

1 can unsweetened sliced apples
½ cup raisins
1 cup rolled oats
½ cup Grapenuts

¼ cup frozen apple juice
concentrate, thawed
2 tbsp. water
cinnamon

Combine oats, Grapenuts, juice concentrate and water. Spread on a baking sheet and toast at 300 degrees until crispy. Combine apples and raisins in a baking dish and sprinkle with cinnamon. Spread oat topping over apple mixture and bake at 350 degrees for 15 minutes. Serve hot.

## TOFU BANANA PUDDING

### SERVINGS: 4

**PREPARATION TIME:** 15 mins. **CHILLING TIME:** 30 mins.

½ lb. tofu
3 bananas
½ cup peanut butter
¼ cup honey

2 tbsp. carob powder
½ tsp. vanilla
dash of cinnamon and nutmeg
  (optional)

Break tofu into chunks and cut bananas into pieces. In a food processor or blender, combine bananas, peanut butter, and honey. Add tofu, a chunk at a time, blending until mixture is smooth like a pudding. If it is too thick, add water, a small amount at a time, until it takes on a pudding consistency. Add remaining ingredients and blend until smooth. Chill at least 30 minutes before serving. (This is a very rich recipe and should be reserved, at most, for an occasional treat.)

# UPDATE ON INGREDIENTS

## OIL-FREE DRESSINGS

There are many oil-free salad dressings available in the supermarket and natural food stores these days. These dressings can add flavor to green salads and potato salads. They can also be used to marinate vegetables such as mushrooms, eggplant, baby corn and carrots, or used as a topping for hot vegetables. Choose brands that are low in salt and other additives. There are also recipes in the McDougall Cookbooks for oil-free dressings.

## PURE VEGETABLE SEASONINGS

Some vegetable seasoning mixes can be used to make an excellent soup base. Bernard Jensen's Broth and Seasoning Mix is a good one that is easy to find. Gaylord Hauser's Vegetable Broth is also acceptable. They can be used to add flavor to soup, stew, gravies or sauces.

## WORCESTERSHIRE

There is a natural Worcestershire sauce on the market that is made without anchovies. All natural ingredients are used. Use this in recipes calling for this type of flavor. Sharwood's Worcestershire Sauce is one acceptable brand. This brand can usually be found in the gourmet section of the supermarket.

## BARBEQUE SAUCE

There are a few commercially available barbeque sauces that are acceptable from a health viewpoint. Be sure to read the labels and choose the ones with no oil and a low-sodium content.

## HORSERADISH

Horseradish should be the pure variety, do not buy the "creamed" varieties. Most supermarkets will carry acceptable brands. People sensitive to hot flavorings should avoid horseradish. There is a Japanese horseradish powder called Wasabiko. Found in Oriental food markets.

## JAPANESE MUSTARD or EUTREMA MUSTARD

It is available in Oriental food stores. People sensitive to hot mustard may be advised to avoid this flavoring. This is sometimes also labeled Wasabiko.

## CHINESE PLUM SAUCE OR UMEBOSHI PLUM SAUCE

Chinese plum sauce is available in some supermarkets and a few natural food stores. The ingredients are natural and will provide an interesting flavor to many vegetable dishes, especially those from your Chinese selection of recipes. You may also find this labeled "Duck Sauce" in the gourmet section of the supermarket. It is interchangeable with Umeboshi Plum Sauce.

## TAMARI OR SOY SAUCE

When a recipe calls for low sodium tamari, shoyu, or soy sauce, these ingredients are all interchangeable. They are all made from soybeans, wheat and salt. Some wheat-free brands are available. You should look for the brands with the lowest sodium content. Also be sure the brand you choose does not contain monosodium glutamate (MSG).

## CELLOPHANE NOODLES

Cellophane Noodles can be found in Oriental food stores. Some supermarkets may also carry them, especially when they have an Oriental section. These noodles are also called bean threads or "long rice". They are made from bean starch and water. They are clear when cooked.

## UDON

Udon are Japanese-style noodles made from buckwheat flour, wheat flour, and water. They are found in natural food stores or in the Oriental section of the supermarket.

## OKARA

Okara is a by-product of tofu making. It is the pulp that is left behind after the soymilk has been pressed from the soybean. This product is white in color and very high in fiber. It may be used to add moisture to baked goods.

## TEMPEH

Tempeh is a cultured soy bean product, made from whole soy beans. It is found in natural food and Oriental stores.

## KOMBU

Kombu is a type of seaweed used mainly to give flavor to soup stock or broth. It can be quite salty, so you may want to rinse it under running water before using a piece of it for soup stock. Look for it in Oriental food markets or natural food stores.

## CHAPATI

Chapati are large flat circles made from whole wheat flour. They resemble Mexican flour tortillas. They may be found in natural food stores and some progressive supermarkets. They are often found frozen.

## TAHINI

Tahini is a nut butter made from sesame seeds. It may be found in natural food stores or possibly the gourmet section of a supermarket. You can make your own Tahini by grinding up sesame seeds and adding a small amount of water to bring to a proper consistency.

## EGG REPLACER

Egg replacer is a product made by Ener-G Foods Inc. It can be ordered by your local health food store or by you personally through the mail by writing P.O. Box 24723, Seattle, WA 98124-0723. This product is used in recipes as a binding agent to replace eggs in baking (not to be confused with anything resembling an egg for eating).

## BAKING POWDER

Baking powder is lower in sodium than baking soda, but still must be considerably limited for those on salt restriction. Aluminum is used as a leavening agent in many brands of baking powder. This metal should be avoided when you choose a baking powder because of the possibility of long term toxicity from aluminum ingestion.

# PREPARED AHEAD RECIPES

Some recipes may be prepared completely ahead of time. The final baking or reheating is done before dinner. This is particularly helpful when you entertain guests for dinner.

Most Soups
Spicy Lentil Filling
Jewish Yam Stew
Tempeh and Grain Casserole
Milton's Special Barbeque
Multiple Bean Casserole
Southern Style Black Eyed Peas
Boston Baked Beans
Bean and Vegetable Casserole
Six-Way-Fun Chili
South American Bean Stew
Fejoiada
Spring Rolls
Seven Layer Casserole
Bean Loaf
Spicy Mixed Bean Chili
Black Bean Chili
Multi Grain Stew
Dilly Stuffed Cabbage

Fruited Rice Stuffing
Rice-Tofu Stuffing
Stuffed Vegetables
Lasagna Roll-ups
Tofu Loaf
Where's The Meat Loaf?
Vegetable Burritos
Stuffed Chapati Rolls
Leafy Green Chapatis
Cold Brown Rice Salad
Vegetable Salad
Linda's Noodle Salad
Colorful Coleslaw
Lentil Salad
Rice and Corn Salad
Super Sprout Salad
Three Bean Salad
Pasta Salad Bowl

## SLOW COOKERS

Some recipes are easy to prepare in a slow cooker. Add all ingredients at once. The amount of water used may have to be reduced by 1 to 2 cups because slow cookers usually do not lose much water while cooking. Times may vary depending on which brand of slow cooker you have. You may need to halve some recipes, if your slow cooker is small.

Simple Vegetable Soup
Mexican Bean Soup
Nine Staples Soup
Six-Way-Fun Chili
Spicy Mixed Bean Chili

Black Bean Chili
Israeli Wheat Berry Stew
Grainy Stew
Multigrain Stew

# QUICK AND EASY RECIPES

Some recipes take less time to prepare than do others and are good for days when you are busy.

Quick Pasta Toss
Thai Basil Pasta
Quick Creamy Vegatables
Chunky A La King Sauce
Chinese Spicy Sauce
Tempeh Creole
Haposai

Italian Cauliflower
Deviled Green Beans
Mexican Corn
Broiled Dijon Tomatoes
Quick Oriental Cabbage
Zucchini Casserole
Ginger Carrots

Summer Stew
Quick Saucy Vegetables
Creamed Curried Vegetables
Spicy Vegetable Sauce
Summer Vegetable Delight
Syrian Bamya
Green Bulgur
Mexican Bulgur
Chinese Vegetables
Buddha's Delight
Italian Dressed Spaghetti
Spinach Tofu Burgers
Pasta Primavera
Oat Burgers
Jim's Breaded Eggplant

Cajun Potatoes
Zucchini-Potato Curry
Mandarin Eggplant
Green Bean Special
Zucchini Velvet Soup
Creamy Thai Soup
Cream of Broccoli Soup
Mushroom Soup
Golden Onion Soup
Carrot Soup
Green Onion Soup
Sherried Tomato Soup
Cellophane Noodle Soup
Miso Soup
Fresh Vegetable Soup

Some recipes are prepared quickly if you have cooked rice or beans in your refrigerator or freezer. On the days that you prepare rice or beans, make some extra and refrigerate or freeze in 2 to 3 cup containers.

Quick Chili
Rice and Corn Salad
Boston Baked Beans
New Orleans Creole Sauce
Quick Rice Dinner
Mexican Rice
Spicy Chinese Rice

Pea and Potato Curry
White Bean Spread
Hummus
Kidney Bean Spread
Spicy Bean Spread
Potatoes with Dill

# 100 DAYS OF DINNER MENU SUGGESTIONS FROM THE MCDOUGALL HEALTH-SUPPORTING COOKBOOKS VOL I & II

Number following recipe denotes book in which recipe can be found:

(1) The McDougall Health-Supporting Cookbook, Vol I
(2) The McDougall Health-Supporting Cookbook, Vol II

Day 1    South of the Border Soup (2)
         Vegetable Burritos (2)

Day 2    Carrot Soup (2)
Pasta Primavera (2)

Day 3    Three Bean Salad (2)
Potatoes with Dill (2)
Broccoli

Day 4    Chinese Hot Salad (1)
Chinese Vegetables (2)
Brown Rice

Day 5    Spinach Salad (1)
Black Bean Chili (2)
Mexican Corn (2)

Day 6    Vegetable Pie (2)
Sweet Potatoes and Apricots (2)

Day 7    Where's the Meat Loaf? (2)
Seasoned Potatoes in Foil (2)
Peas

Day 8    Italian Dressed Spaghetti (2)
Jim's Breaded Eggplant (2)

Day 9    Butch's Bean Soup (1)
Baked Potato Salad (2)

Day 10    Lima Beans Salad (2)
Chapati (2)*
Fruited Rice Stuffing (2)

Day 11    Sprout Salad (1)
Mary's Minestrone (1)

Day 12    Quick Pasta Toss (2)
Wicked Mushrooms (1)
Baked Potatoes

Day 13    TVP Sloppy Joe's (1)
Whole Wheat Buns
Assorted Garnishes

Day 14    Sweet-Sour Vegetables Saute (1)
Brown Rice
Chinese Cabbage with Bean Sprouts (1)

*Chapati may be purchased in natural food stores and some progressive supermarkets. They resemble a whole wheat tortilla.

Day 15    Calico Soup (1)
          Tomato-Onion Cucumber Salad (1)
          Muffins (1)

Day 16    Lentil Salad (2)
          Crazy Layered Noodles (1)
          Dijon Tomatoes (2)

Day 17    Autumn Barley Stew (1)
          Spicy Green Beans (1)
          Pineapple Muffins (2)

Day 18    Black Bean Soup (1)
          Lee's Cabbage Salad (1)
          Pita Bread (1)*

Day 19    Jewish Yam Stew (2)
          Saucy Brussels Sprouts (2)

Day 20    Pea and Potato Curry (2)
          Cauliflower Curry (1)
          Indian Cabbage (1)

Day 21    Chunky A'la King Sauce (2)
          Whole Wheat Toast
          Green Salad (1)

Day 22    Oriental Dressed Noodles (2)
          Zucchini Casserole (2)

Day 23    Oat Burgers (2)
          Whole Wheat Buns
          Assorted Garnishes
          Lentil Salad (2)

Day 24    Winter Grains Soup (2)
          Colorful Coleslaw (2)

Day 25    Six Way Fun Chili (2)
          Brown Rice
          Corn

Day 26    Yam and Apple Casserole (1)
          Mediterranean Mushrooms (1)
          Rice and Corn Salad (2)


*Pita bread may be purchased in most supermarkets and natural food stores.
Look for the whole wheat variety.

Day 27    Polenta Pie (1)
          Broiled Zucchini (1)

Day 28    Lentil Loaf (1)
          Mushroom Gravy (1)
          Herbed Green Beans (1)

Day 29    Italian Pasta Soup (2)
          Sprouted Lettuce Salad (1)

Day 30    Mushroom Curry (1)
          Spicy Green Beans (1)
          Brown Rice-long grain

Day 31    Malterre's Millet Loaf (1)
          Sweet Corn
          Green Salad

Day 32    Janine's Spaghetti Sauce (2)
          Spaghetti Noodles
          French Bread with Garlic Spread (1)

Day 33    Moroccan Stew (2)
          Quick Pasta Toss (2)

Day 34    Wild Rice Soup (2)
          New Potato Salad (1)

Day 35    White Mushroom Sauce (1)
          Whole Wheat Noodles
          Spinach Salad (1)

Day 36    Quick Confetti Rice (1)
          Baked Winter Squash (1)

Day 37    Multi Grain Stew (2)
          Carrot Orange Salad (2)
          Muffins (1)

Day 38    Spaghetti Squash Surprise (1)
          Tomato-Mushroom Casserole (1)

Day 39    Country Vegetable Soup (2)
          Linda's Noodle Salad (2)
          Pita Bread(1)

Day 40    Grainy Mushrooms (1)
          Mashed Stuffed Squash (2)
          Vegetable Salad (2)

Day 41     Milton's Special Barbeque (2)
           Whole Wheat Buns or Bread
           Assorted Garnishes

Day 42     Creamy Thai Soup (2)
           Buddha's Delight (2)
           Quick Oriental Cabbage (2)

Day 43     Curried Chapati Roll-ups (1)
           Simple Baked Eggplant (1)

Day 44     Green Salad (1)
           Oil-free Dressing (1)
           Potato-Veggie Dinner (2)
           Creamy Mushroom Sauce (2)

Day 45     Summer Vegetable Delight (2)
           Super Sprout Salad (2)

Day 46     Miso Soup (2)
           Japanese Udon and Vegetables (2)

Day 47     Bean Loaf (2)
           Sauce (1)
           Italian Cauliflower (2)

Day 48     Spicy Chinese Rice (2)
           Mandarin Eggplant (2)

Day 49     Mexican Gazpacho (2)
           Potato Salad (1)

Day 50     Lasagna Roll-ups (2)
           Lemon broccoli (2)

Day 51     Spicy Vegetable Sauce (2)
           Brown Rice
           Steamed Vegetables

Day 52     Lima Bean Jambalaya (1)
           Pita Bread (1)
           Steamed Greens (2)

Day 53     Vegetable Salad (2)
           Curried Pumpkin Soup (2)

Day 54     Greek Stew (2)
           Mashed Potatoes (1)
           Gourmet Crookneck Squash (2)

Day 55    Boston Baked Beans (2)
          Vegetables A'la Grecque (2)

Day 56    Mushroom Soup (2)
          Leafy Green Chapatis (2)

Day 57    Haposai (2)
          Brown Rice
          Silva's Soba Noodle Salad (1)

Day 58    New Orleans Creole Sauce (2)
          Whole Grain Pasta
          Deviled Green Beans (2)

Day 59    Colombian Dinner Soup (2)
          Spinach Salad (1)

Day 60    Falafel (2)
          Whole Wheat Pita Bread (1)
          Assorted Garnishes

Day 61    Luau Rice (2)
          Garbanzo Salad (2)

Day 62    Pasta and Fagioli (2)
          Boiled Dijon Tomatoes (2)

Day 63    Spicy Lentil Filling (2)
          Chapatis (2)
          Assorted Garnishes

Day 64    Green Bulgur (2)
          Syrian Potato Salad (2)

Day 65    Southern Style Black Eyed Peas (2)
          Ginger Carrots (2)

Day 66    Curried Vegetable Stew (1)
          Brown Rice
          India Eggplant (2)

Day 67    Green Onion Soup (2)
          Rice and Corn Salad (2)

Day 68    Multiple Bean Casserole (2)
          Zesty Peppers (1)

Day 69    Seven Layer Casserole (2)
          Tossed Green Salad

Day 70    African Millet and Beans (2)
          Sauteed Mushrooms (2)

Day 71    Quick Saucy Vegetables (2)
          Whole Wheat Bread
          Pasta Salad Bowl (2)

Day 72    Summertime Chowder (1)
          Potato Salad (1)

Day 73    Polynesian Vegetables (1)
          Twice Baked Potatoes (1)
          Chinese Peas and Mushrooms (1)

Day 74    Israeli Wheat Berry Stew (2)
          Vegetable Melage (1)

Day 75    Hot Yammy Soup (1)
          Spinach Salad (1)
          Muffins (1)

Day 76    Pasta Salad Bowl (2)
          Cajun Potatoes (2)
          Broccoli

Day 77    Spicy Mixed Bean Chili (2)
          Colcannon (2)
          Marinated Cucumbers (2)

Day 78    Mushroom Strogonoff (2)
          Flat Noodles
          Saucy Brussels Sprouts (2)

Day 79    Quick Brown Stew (1)
          Brown Rice
          Zucchini Casserole (2)

Day 80    Grainy Vegetable Soup (1)
          Sprouted Lettuce Salad (1)

Day 81    Mungo Beans (2)
          Cornmeal Rice Patties (1)
          Italian Cauliflower (2)

Day 82    Beanoodle Casserole (2)
          Lee's Cabbage Salad (1)

Day 83    Lima Bean Chowder (2)
          Vegetable Salad Provencale (1)

Day 84    Grainy Vegetable Stew (2)
          Lemon Broccoli (2)

Day 85    Quick Chili (2)
          Baked Potato
          Green Bean Special (2)

Day 86    Country Soup (1)
          Mung Bean Sprout Salad (1)

Day 87    Summer Stew (2)
          Whole Grain Noodles
          Lentil Salad (2)

Day 88    Mexican Rice (2)
          Zucchini-Corn Casserole (2)
          Green Salad

Day 89    Chapatis (2)
          Refried Beans (1)
          Assorted Chopped Vegetables
          Salsas (2)

Day 90    Zucchini Velvet Soup (2)
          Dilly Stuffed Cabbage (2)

Day 91    South American Bean Stew (2)
          Sweet potato
          Spinach Salad (1)

Day 92    Layered Rice Casserole (1)
          Three Bean Salad (2)

Day 93    Hearty Potato Vegetable Curry (2)
          Baked Potato
          Lima Bean Salad (2)

Day 94    Spanish Garbanzo Soup (2)
          Vegetables A'la Grecque (2)

Day 95    Black Beans with Nectarines (2)
          Brown Rice
          Tossed Green Salad (1)

Day 96    Chunky Vegetable Sauce (1)
          Barley-Mushroom Casserole (1)
          Macroni Salad (1)

Day 97    Mexican Bulgar (2)
          Assorted Garnishes
          Chapati (2)
          Corn Tortillas

Day 98    Gnocchi (2)
          Spaghetti Sauce (1)
          Steamed Vegetable Salad (1)

Day 99    North African Bean Soup (2)
          Cajun Potatoes (2)
          Peas

Day 100   Garbanzo Stew (1)
          Brown Rice (1)
          Shredded Salad (1)

# BUFFET PARTY IDEAS

**APPETIZERS:**

Apply a layer of spicy bean spread on slices of fresh vegetables, such as zucchini rounds, cucumber rounds, celery stalks sliced in two pieces, and many other tasty vegetables. You can use a pastry bag with a decorative tip and pipe onto the vegetables. Garnish with olive slivers, pimiento, or parsley. This is also an excellent idea for interesting bread toppings. Cut slices of bread into decorative shapes and top as directed above. Some delicious bean spreads to try are: Kidney Bean Spread, Hummus, Lentil-Mushroom Pate, Spicy Bean Spread or White Bean Spread (all of these recipes are found in the McDougall cookbooks).

There are many excellent crackers available in stores that are made without oil. Some examples are: Crispy Cakes, Brown Rice Crackers, Kavli Norwegian Flatbread, Wasa, Unseasoned Rye Krisp, and others made primarily from whole grain flour and few additives. You can make your own from corn tortillas or pita bread (instructions are in The McDougall Plan.) Serve these with any of the bean spreads listed above, or with an assortment of the tofu dips in Volumes I and II of the cookbooks.

A fresh vegetable platter is also a good choice for an appetizer tray. Choose an assortment of as many vegetables as you desire. Try using old favorites and some new ones that you haven't considered before, such as:

snow peas, asparagus, broccoli, zucchini, mushrooms, cauliflower, green beans, carrots and celery. Serve with an assortment of sauces for dipping, like Salsa Cruda, Avocado Salsa, Hot Peanut Dip, tofu dips, or one of your favorites.

Other delicious appetizer choices found in the cookbooks are: Sushi, Stuffed Mushroom Caps, Marinated Mushrooms, Dolmas, and Manapua.

## SALADS:

Some salads are perfect to serve at a party for guests to eat and can be served buffet style. Serve as many as you wish, depending on your guest list.

Fruit Salad (1)
Steamed Vegetable Salad (1)
Potato Salad (1)
Macaroni Salad (1)
Tabouli (MP)
Super Sprout Salad (2)
Pasta Salads (2)
Three Bean Salad (2)
Lentil Salad (2)
Vegetable Salad (2)
Rice and Corn Salad (2)
Garbanzo Salad (2)

## MAIN DISHES:

Main dishes at a buffet party should be kept simple and easy for your guests to eat using only a fork. Choose as many as you wish, but choose a wide variety from bean dishes, grain dishes and vegetable dishes.

| | |
|---|---|
| Bean: | Boston Baked Beans (2) |
| | Cajun Bean Stew (2) |
| | Black Bean Chili (2) |
| | Curried Garbanzos (1) |
| | Baked Beans (1) |
| | Elaine's Spicy Lentils (1) |
| Grains: | Green Bulgur (2) |
| | Israeli Wheat Berry Stew (2) |
| | Wild Rice Casserole (2) |
| | Mexican Rice (2) |
| | Spicy Chinese Rice (2) |
| | Savory Brown Rice (1) |
| | Malterre's Millet Loaf (1) |
| | Grainy Mushrooms (1) |

Vegetables:  Pea and Potato Curry (2)
Buddha's Delight (2)
Yam N Apple Casserole (1)
Mandarin Eggplant (2)
Szechuan Shish-Kebabs (1)
Crazy Layered Noodles (1)

## DESSERTS:

Desserts should be easy to cut into small pieces and pick up with the fingers to eat. Choose as many as you wish.

Rich Moist Fruit Cake (1)
Carrot Cake (2)
Apple-Carob Cake (1)
Apple Raisin Bars (1)
Banana Bread (1)
Brownies (1)
Okara Cookies (2)
Apple Bran Cake (2)
Banana-Raisin Cookies (2)

## MENUS FOR DINNER PARTIES FROM VOLUME II

1. Creamy Thai Soup
   Fejoiada
   Vegetable Salad
   Peach Pie

2. Gourmet Onion Soup
   Leafy Green Chapatis
   Apricot Chutney Sauce
   Broiled Dijon Tomatoes
   Lentil Salad
   Berry Sorbet

3. Mushroom Soup
   Six-Way-Fun Chili -
   Pasta Salad Bowl
   Zucchini Casserole
   Carrot Cake

4. Cellophane Noodle Soup
   Buddha's Delight
   Spicy Chinese Rice
   Mandarin Eggplant
   Fruit Ice

5. Zucchini Velvet Soup
   Lasagna Roll-ups
   Three Bean Salad
   Saucy Brussels Sprouts or Lemon Broccoli
   Whole Wheat Crepe with Fruit Sauce

6. White Onion Bisque
   Vegetable of your choice stuffed with TVP Stuffing Mix
   Vegetables A La Grecque
   Sauteed Mushrooms
   Super Sprout Salad
   Apple Pie

# FAVORITE DISHES OF MEMBERS OF THE MCDOUGALL FAMILY

Listed here are some of the favorite recipes of members of the McDougall Family. Most of those listed are enjoyed by everyone. These should give you some ideas on what your children might like and also you might find someone in our family that shares similar taste in foods with you.

Source of recipe indicated by Parenthesis:

(MP) The McDougall Plan
(1) The McDougall Health-Supporting Cookbook Vol I
(2) The McDougall Health-Supporting Cookbook Vol II

## CRAIG (age 3):

Potato Salad (1)
Seasoned Potatoes in Foil (2)
Oat Burgers (2)
Yam N Apple Casserole (1)
Pasta Salad (2)
Cashew French Toast (2)
Where's The Meat Loaf? (2)
Beans and Chapaties (MP)
Bean Enchiladas (MP)
Spaghetti and Marinara Sauce (MP)

**PATRICK (age 11):**

Refried Beans and Chips (MP)
White Bean Soup (MP)
Pat's Favorite Pancakes (2)
Mashed Potatoes (1)
Apple Carob Cake (1)
Golden Potatoes (MP)
Marinara Sauce with Noodles (MP)
Lasagna Roll-ups (2)
Boston Baked Beans (2)
Chapatis and Refried Beans (MP)


**HEATHER (age 12):**

Six-Way-Fun Chili (2)
Quick Pasta Toss (2)
Malterre's Millet Loaf (1)
Spring Rolls (2)
Manapua (2)
Heather's Mushroom Delight (MP)
Apple Pancakes (1)
Wilted Lettuce (1)
Mexican Corn Bread (1)
Pizza (MP)


**MARY:**

Israeli Wheat Berry Stew (2)
Creamy Thai Soup (2)
Chunky A' La King Sauce (2)
Leafy Green Chapatis (2)
Mandarin Eggplant (2)
Columbian Dinner Soup (2)
Lentil-Mushroom Pate (2)
Easy Curried Pea Soup (MP)
Vegetable Curry (MP)
Summer Time Chowder (1)


**JOHN:**

Garbanzo Stew (1)
Brazilian Black Beans with Marinated Tomatoes (MP)
Japanese Udon with Vegetables (2)

Chili (MP)
TVP Sloppy Joes (1)
Fried Rice (MP)
Green Rice (MP)
Corn and Potato Soup (1)
Lentil Dahl and Chapaties (1)
Stuffed Cabbage Rolls (MP)

# MICROWAVE COOKING

Microwave cooking is a moist cooking method. The best recipes to convert to microwave cooking are saucy dishes and stews, casseroles that are covered during cooking, or vegetables that are steamed.

To adapt recipes in the McDougall books to microwave cooking follow these simple suggestions for best results:

TIME: Most cooking times can be reduced by ⅔ to ¾. Start by cooking the food only ¼ as long as stated in the recipe. Test for doneness. If it needs more cooking time, increase in small amounts.

LIQUID: Very little evaporation occurs in microwave cooking, so you will need less liquid than the recipe calls for. Reduce the amount of liquid by about ¼.

REST TIME: Microwaved food continues to cook after it is removed from the oven. By allowing foods enough rest time you will make sure they are completely cooked.

COVER: Be sure to cover all foods that you cook in the microwave. This will hold in steam and help foods cook faster without drying out.

STIR: When cooking saucy dishes and stews, stir the food occasionally to redistribute the heat.

ROTATE: When cooking casseroles or other foods that cannot be stirred, then rotate the cooking dish several times during cooking to help heat it evenly.

SAFETY: Much research has been done on the safety of microwave cooking and the ovens. The microwave heating process results in foods with as high a nutrient content (and sometimes higher) as conventional ovens.

The FDA believes that microwave ovens are safe in the household as long as they have not suffered damage that results in leakage. Check the door seal occasionally with a radiation leakage detector. Do not operate the oven if the door does not close properly. Be sure to follow the manufacturer's operation instructions.

The advantages of a microwave are cost and time savings. However, these must be weighed against the potential hazards of microwave leakage. I find that a microwave is very handy for reheating foods, cooking frozen vegetables, boiling water, baking one or two potatoes, and other simple uses.

# INDEX

# The McDougall Books

THE MCDOUGALL PLAN—Learn how to successfully live by a health-supporting diet and lifestyle, shop, meal plan, and eat out, with 108 recipes.

MCDOUGALL'S MEDICINE—A CHALLENGING SECOND OPINION—Here are the reasons why present therapies are not improving or prolonging lives for most people. There is a way for prevention and help for the victims of cancer, osteoporosis, atherosclerosis, heart disease (bypass surgery), hypertension, diabetes, arthritis, and kidney disease.

THE MCDOUGALL HEALTH-SUPPORTING COOKBOOKS, VOLUMES I & II—Each volume contains 250 original recipes from health-supporting (category IV) to many with richer ingredients (category III). Includes desserts, gluten-free recipes, party plans and suggestions for children.

These books can be purchased in better book stores throughout the country. However, further information and assistance in finding books can be obtained by writing John McDougall, M.D., P.O. Box 14039, Santa Rosa, CA 95402.

## The McDougall Live-In Health Program

Dr. McDougall is the medical director of the live-in lifestyle/nutrition program at St. Helena Hospital & Health Center, Deer Park, CA 94576. Health facilities in other areas of the country are planned to open in the future. This program is designed to help people discontinue medications, avoid surgeries when possible, regain lost health and appearance through sensible changes in diet and personal habits, and maintain good health. More information can be obtained by writing John McDougall, M.D. at P.O. Box 14039, Santa Rosa, CA 95402.

## Newsletter and Tapes

Information on subscribing to a newsletter to keep you up to date on timely medical information, important health events throughout the country, and new recipes produced by the McDougalls can be obtained by writing them at P.O. Box 14039, Santa Rosa, CA 95402.

A professionally produced album of eight audio tapes by Dr. McDougall and his staff is also available that will inform and inspire you change your diet and your life, forever.